Contents

Thomas Chatterton by Henry Wallis (1856). In 1770 Chatterton, a talented writer, killed himself with arsenic. He was only 17. His torn-up manuscripts litter the floor. Another poet, George Meredith, posed as Chatterton for Wallis.

Introduction

Poems and poets

Poets' lives can seem very striking and haunting. Certain scenes stay in the mind: Byron watching Shelley's body dissolve in the furnace flames on the Italian beach, seeing it as 'a satire on our pride and folly'; Keats listening to the nightingale in Hampstead and scribbling his ode 'on some scraps of paper'; Wilfred Owen, his 'senses charred' in battle in October 1918, supporting a dying soldier 'whose blood lies yet crimson on my shoulder'; William and Dorothy Wordsworth, on a day so windy they could not catch their breaths, coming upon thousands of wild daffodils that 'tossed and reeled and danced' beside Lake Ullswater; Coleridge sitting down to write out his opium-inspired dream poem, only to be interrupted by the 'person from Porlock'; the blind Milton dictating *Paradise Lost* to his daughters; Burns ploughing up a mouse's nest in the autumn fields; 12-year-old Alexander Pope respectfully admiring the elderly Dryden at White's Coffee House; and Thomas Gray peering at gravestones in Stoke Poges churchyard at twilight.

The glamour of the stories tends to obscure what poets do less glamorously: think and write. Many people dislike poets. Their mental image of them is that of Thomas Chatterton in Henry Wallis's Victorian painting: the poet – young, fancily dressed, long-haired, incapable of earning a living – poses even in death, surrounded by scribbled scraps of writing that have no use or merit. In fact, any genuine poet's manuscripts tell a very different story: that poetry is hard work. The old word for poet – 'maker' – gives a better picture of a craftsman with words, constantly reworking to refine and improve. Even William Blake, whose words are like the mystic sayings of some great prophet, can be seen in the manuscripts sharpening and developing that apparently superhuman poem, *The tyger*.

Poetry is also deeply influential, providing the most enduring, precious record of the times in which the poets lived. Shabby Keats, and Wordsworth sitting on his wall by Dove Cottage, tell us far more about their eras than any records of the now forgotten, more conventional people who lived then and no doubt despised the very idea of 'poet'. Shelley called poets the 'unacknowledged legislators of the world'. They are more. They sum up the 'spirit of the age' and allow us to see and understand our history.

Poets also tell us about ourselves. They put into words what most of us feel about our lives. Like Shakespeare, we watch the waves on the beach and think that they are like the minutes relentlessly passing; like Tennyson, we wonder, when someone close to us dies, whether life has any meaning, or whether it is all pointless; like Burns, we bitterly reflect on the way we treat fellow living creatures on the planet; like Shelley, we rage about the tyranny of cruel governments; unhappily in love, we feel, like the Renaissance poets with their hunting images, as if we were hopelessly chasing the elusive loved one through the forests of life.

The great Romantic poets give us some attractive definitions of poetry and poets. Here are some of them. John Keats says that the poet has the gift to express the things we all feel about ourselves and about life: 'poetry should strike the reader as a wording of his own highest thoughts, and appear almost as a remembrance'. Samuel Coleridge sees poetry as the most effective way of expressing ideas, thoughts and feelings, using the full resources of the language to do so: 'the best words in the best order'. Shelley tells us how poetry can increase our delight in the world around us: 'poetry lifts the veil from the hidden beauty of the world, and makes familiar objects be as if they were not familiar'. William Wordsworth asks:

> What is a poet? ... He is a man speaking to men, a man ... endued with more lively sensibility, more enthusiasm and tenderness, who has a greater knowledge of human nature, and a more comprehensive soul, than are supposed to be common among mankind ... and who rejoices more than other men in the spirit of life that is within him ... and, from practice, has acquired a greater readiness and power in expressing what he thinks and feels.

Wordsworth offers a clear picture of the poet as a spokesman for our own thoughts. Finding the words for this is his or her particular genius, and success in this makes poetry, as A. E. Housman noted, 'the highest form of literature'.

Using the collection

This book introduces English poetry to the secondary school student. It is based on the National Curriculum prescription: all the pre-20th-century poets on the set list (except Chaucer) are here, as are four 20th-century poets 'with well established critical reputations'.

I am sad to leave out so many wonderful poets: Crabbe, Goldsmith, Wilde and Johnson, for example, or the captivating women writers of the 18th and 19th centuries, recently 'rediscovered', and the minor figures that are such a vital part of English literature, the kind of poet Longfellow had in mind when he put aside the 'grand old masters' to read

> Some humbler poet
> Whose songs gushed from his heart,
> As showers from the clouds of summer
> Or tears from the eyelids start!

But then, a book, like a set list, can only contain so much.

The notes and questions suggest ways into the poems. The most demanding pieces obviously need more. Donne, Marvell and Vaughan, for example, really need to be read intensively with the Bible and Greek myths beside us. Many poems, however, can give pleasure and interest to readers of all abilities. The short questions are for discussion or written comprehension. Substantial ideas for written work are indicated with the symbol **W** . The symbol **D** denotes suggestions suitable for oral work. Analysis can be satisfying, but imaginative responses, in poetry as well as prose, can be equally stimulating: poets themselves have imitated their predecessors creatively across the centuries. The illustrations bring to life the poets and their intellectual and cultural backgrounds, and can be used to encourage students' written and spoken work. Words that are defined in the glossary at the back of the book are marked in bold, for example, **IRONY**.

Byron in Venice
Scratching up his ideas
(1823).

•PART 1•

Tudor and Jacobean poetry

1 Sir Thomas Wyatt (?1503-1542): The slipper top of court's estates

Wyatt became an important official at the court of King Henry VIII. This was a splendid but dangerous life. To fall from favour could mean imprisonment, torture and beheading. Wyatt was imprisoned several times, falsely accused by court enemies, and only just escaped execution in 1541. His diplomatic travels took him to France and Italy, and his love of writing led him to study French and Italian poetry. From the great Italian poets Dante (1265-1321) and Petrarch (1304-1374) he borrowed the sonnet form and was the first poet to use it in English.

Sir Thomas Wyatt by Hans Holbein (1528). The tensions of life at Henry VIII's court are expressed in the guarded looks of the courtier.

Wyatt died of a fever contracted after an over-long ride in the King's service. His poems were read only in manuscript form during his life, and were not printed until several years after his death. An important **THEME** in his poetry is the uncertainty of life in the court of a cruel, fickle tyrant like Henry VIII. Here is an **EPIGRAM** about court life.

Epigram: Stand whoso list

Stand whoso list[1] upon the slipper[2] top
Of court's estates,[3] and let me here rejoice
And use me quiet without let[4] or stop,
Unknown in court that hath such brackish[5] joys.
In hidden place so let my days forth pass
That, when my years be done withouten noise,
I may die aged after the common trace.[6]
For him death grip'th right hard by the crop[7]
That is much known of other, and of himself, alas,
Doth die unknown, dazed, with dreadful face.

[1] let whoever wants to, stand   [2] slippery   [3] a place at court   [4] obstruction   [5] over-salted   [6] like ordinary people   [7] throat

This poem is translated from the Latin of the Roman poet Seneca, but Wyatt has added his own details, such as the ghastly face of the execution victim, something that he had seen many times.

Look at the first line. Wyatt compares a courtier to someone on top of a slippery roof. Another version has 'upon the slipper wheel'. Which is better?
Where does the courtier long to be? What sort of life is he anxious to have?
'Much known of other' means famous. What sort of death lies ahead for a famous person who has fallen from power?
How has fame damaged the poet's soul?

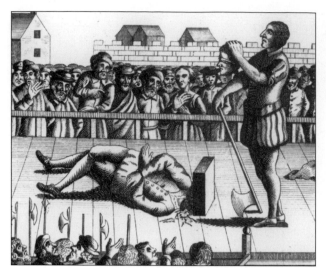

Public execution of a statesman at the Tower of London. The heads of such 'traitors' were then displayed on London Bridge.

The contrast between life in court and out of it is an important theme in 16th-century writing. Robert Devereux, Earl of Essex (?1566-1601), was a favourite of Queen Elizabeth I. He fell from power and was executed for treason. He wrote this poem just before he died.

Happy were he

Happy were he could finish forth his fate[1]
  In some unhaunted[2] desert, most obscure[3]
From all societies, from love and hate
  Of wordly folk; then might he sleep secure;
Then wake again, and give God ever praise,
  Content with hips and haws[4] and bramble-berry;
In contemplation spending all his days,
  And change of holy thoughts to make him merry;
Where, when he dies, his tomb may be a bush,
Where harmless robin dwells with gentle thrush.

[1] lead the rest of his life   [2] deserted   [3] hidden and remote   [4] the fruit of the rose and hawthorn

What are seen as the worst aspects of court service?
What kind of life does the poet long for?
Which lines are most moving?

W   Write about these poems on 16th-century court life. What good and bad aspects are mentioned? Which poem is more vivid and why?

D   Discuss the execution shown in the picture above. Create a **MONOLOGUE** based on the victim's last thoughts, or on the reflections of a member of the crowd.

Love could also be dangerous for the courtier. Married at 17, Wyatt separated from his wife in 1625, having begun a love affair with Anne Boleyn, one of Queen Catherine's ladies-in-waiting. King Henry himself, however, courted and married Anne

in 1533. Some critics think that the following poem, based on Petrarch's work, refers to Wyatt's broken romance with her.

Sonnet: Who list to hunt

Whoso list[1] to hunt, I know where is an hind,[2]
But as for me, helas,[3] I may no more.
The vain travail[4] hath wearied me so sore,
I am of them that farthest cometh behind.
Yet may I by no means my wearied mind
Draw from the deer, but as she fleeth afore
Fainting I follow. I leave off therefore
Sithens[5] in a net I seek to hold the wind.
Who list her hunt, I put him out of doubt,
As well as I may spend his time in vain.
And graven[6] with diamonds[7] in letters plain
There is written her fair neck round about:
'*Noli me tangere*[8] for Caesar's[9] I am,
And wild for to hold though I seem tame.'

[1] whoever wants   [2] female deer   [3] alas
[4] useless effort   [5] since   [6] set   [7] (**SYMBOLS** of chastity)
[8] (Latin for 'Do not touch me')   [9] Henry VIII's

Courtship was often compared to a hunt in the Petrarchan **SONNET**. Trace the idea of the hunted female deer through the poem.
How does each stage of the hunt reflect the poet's courtship? Where does the net fit in?
Others hunt the hind, too. What is the poet's warning to them?

When Anne fell from favour, she and her supposed lovers, including Wyatt, were imprisoned in the Tower of London. He watched her execution from his cell.

Anne Boleyn, the second of Henry VIII's six wives, by Hans Holbein. Wyatt, her former lover, watched her execution from his cell in the Tower of London.

They flee from me

They flee from me that sometime[1] did me seek
With naked foot stalking in my chamber.
I have seen them gentle, tame, and meek
That now are wild and do not remember
That sometime they put themself in danger
To take bread at my hand; and now they range[2]
Busily seeking with a continual change.

Thanked be fortune it hath been otherwise
Twenty times better, but once in special,[3]
In thin array after a pleasant guise,[4]
When her loose gown from her shoulders did fall
And she me caught in her arms long and small,[5]
Therewithal[6] sweetly did me kiss
And softly said, 'Dear heart, how like you this?'

It was no dream: I lay broad waking.
But all is turned thorough[7] my gentleness
Into a strange fashion of forsaking.[8]
And I have leave to go of her[9] goodness
And she also to use newfangleness.[10]
But since that I so kindly[11] am served[12]
I would fain[13] know what she hath deserved.

[1] at one time [2] move away [3] in particular
[4] in an attractive fashion [5] slender [6] and also
[7] because of [8] giving up [9] as a result of
[10] to be unfaithful [11] typically of the way people behave
[12] treated [13] like to

What comparisons are made to describe the women in the first verse?
Which words create the comparisons?
What is unusual about the roles of the lovers in the second verse?
What details make the girl attractive?
How does the relationship end?
Which words are sarcastic in the last verse?
What does the last line mean?

W Write about Wyatt's attitudes to love in these two poems. What are its joys and difficulties? Comment on the words and comparisons used.

2 Edmund Spenser (1552-1599): Three *Amoretti*

Sir Philip Sidney (1554-1586) started the **SONNET** craze of the 1590s with his sequence *Astrophel and Stella*, and more than 20 sonnet sequences were written in the next 10 years. Sidney borrowed his situation from Petrarch: the adoring Astrophel courts the 'fair cruel', the distant, unresponsive Stella. English poets enjoyed the tight form: 'Is it not most delightful', wrote a sonneteer, Samuel Daniel, 'to see much excellently ordered in a small room?' The heroines of the sequences were not real, nor were the experiences necessarily those of the poets. Elizabethans delighted in the skill required to re-use stock ideas borrowed from Petrarch: the lover as a huntsman, or a soldier attacking a fortress; the lover burning with the fire of love, or wounded by Cupid's arrows. To Elizabethans, the success of the sonnet rested on the skill with which the **CONCEIT** is worked out.

Spenser, who was born in London and made his name as a writer in the household of the Earl of Leicester, joined in the fashion with his *Amoretti*

('little love songs') of 1595. He was sent to Ireland to help the English crush the Irish rebellion. He described the rebels creeping out of the woods to surrender: 'They looked like death. They spoke like ghosts crying out of their graves. They did eat the dead ...'. He lived in a half-ruined castle near Cork, where he was visited by Sir Walter Raleigh (?1552-1618), who was impressed by the opening of his **ALLEGORICAL EPIC**, *The Faerie Queene*. He presented Spenser to Queen Elizabeth, but no court post resulted. When Spenser's Irish home and, it is said, the last parts of *The Faerie Queene*, were destroyed by the rebels, he was forced back to London, where he died. At his funeral in Westminster Abbey, 'mournful **ELEGIES** with the pens that wrote them were thrown into the tomb'.

The *Amoretti* sequence is unusual because it reflects Spenser's actual courtship of his second wife, Elizabeth Boyle. The lover is not left in despair, but marries his mistress, celebrating this in the *Epithalamion* ('a marriage hymn').

Amoretti: Sonnet 30

My love is lyke to yse, and I to fyre:
  how comes it then that this her cold so great
  is not dissolv'd through my so hot desyre,
  but harder growes the more I her intreat?[1]
Or how comes it that my exceeding heat
  is not delayed by her hart frosen cold,
  but that I burne much more in boyling sweat,
  and feele my flames augmented manifold?[2]
What more miraculous thing may be told
  that fire, which all thing melts, should harden yse:
  and yse which is congeald[3] with sencelesse cold,
  should kindle fyre by wonderfull devyse?[4]
Such is the powre of love in gentle mind
  that it can alter all the course of kynd.[5]

[1] beg her (to love me) [2] increased many times
[3] becomes solid [4] method [5] nature

A miniature by Nicholas Hilliard. The flames stand for the torments of unhappy love.

Spenser uses intricate **VERSE FORMS** and deliberately **ARCHAIC DICTION** (for example, his spelling is old-fashioned on purpose), which may prevent him being a popular poet, but he has always been loved by other writers, such as Wordsworth.

What is is the basic idea behind the conceit? Trace its development.

The conceit is an **OXYMORON**, where opposite ideas are put side by side. What clever contrasts does this provide in the poem?

Amoretti: Sonnet 54

Of this worlds Theatre in which we stay,
  My love lyke the Spectator ydly sits
  beholding me that all the pageants[1] play,
  disguysing diversly[2] my troubled wits.
Sometimes I joy when glad occasion fits,[3]
  and mask in myrth[4] lyke to a Comedy:
  soone after when my joy to sorrow flits,
  I waile and make my woes a Tragedy.
Yet she beholding me with constant[5] eye,
  delights not in my merth nor rues my smart:[6]
  but when I laugh she mocks, and when I cry
  she laughes, and hardens evermore her hart.
What then can move her? if nor merth nor mone,[7]
  she is no woman, but a sencelesse stone.

[1] roles [2] in different ways [3] provides an opportunity
[4] put on a comic mask [5] unchanging [6] pities my pain
[7] sadness

What is the conceit in this sonnet and how does Spenser work out the details in each **QUATRAIN**? What conclusion is reached in the **COUPLET**?

D The poem below was written by Sir Walter Raleigh while he was imprisoned in the Tower of London. He and Spenser compare life to a theatre. What other comparisons could you think of to describe life? After your discussion, you could turn your ideas into a poem.

What is our life?

What is our life? A play of passion,
Our mirth the music of division.[1]
Our mother's wombs the tiring-houses[2] be,
Where we are dressed for this short comedy.
Heaven the judicious[3] sharp spectator is,
That sits and marks still who doth act amiss.[4]
Our graves that hide us from the searching sun
Are like drawn curtains when the play is done.
Thus march we, playing, to our latest rest,
Only we die in earnest,[5] that's no jest.

[1] orchestra [2] dressing rooms [3] shrewdly judging
[4] behaves badly [5] in reality

Amoretti: Sonnet 67

Lyke as a huntsman after weary chace,
   Seeing the game from him escapt away,
   sits downe to rest him in some shady place,
   with panting hounds beguilèd[1] of their pray:
So after long pursuit and vaine assay,[2]
   when I all weary had the chace forsooke,
   the gentle deare returned the selfe-same way,
   thinking to quench her thirst at the next brooke.
There she beholding me with mylder looke,
   sought not to fly, but fearelesse still did bide:[3]
   till I in hand her yet halfe trembling tooke,
   and with her owne goodwill hir fyrmely tyde.
Strange thing me seemd[4] to see a beast so wyld,
   so goodly wonne with her owne will beguyld.[1]

[1] tricked [2] pointless effort [3] await [4] it seemed to me

Follow the comparison suggested by the play on the words 'dear' and 'deer', through the poem.

Most sonnet heroines remain cold and aloof. Why is this one different?

W Write about the three *Amoretti*, describing their ideas about love and their use of conceits. Which do you like best?

An unknown poet: a miniature by Nicholas Hilliard.

3 William Shakespeare (1564-1616): His sugared sonnets

Shakespeare was born in Stratford-Upon-Avon, Warwickshire, which he left some time after his early marriage to Anne Hathaway in 1582, to make his fortune in London. In 1592 a jealous rival writer described Shakespeare as an 'upstart crow ... the only Shake-scene in a country', which shows that he had become a successful dramatist at the new theatres in London. When London theatres were closed by outbreaks of plague, Shakespeare turned to poetry. The Earl of Southampton, a 19-year-old rising star at court, was the patron of such **NARRATIVE** poems as *Venus and Adonis* and *The Rape of Lucrece* (1593-1594).

Much of Shakespeare's **SONNET** sequence probably also dates from the 1590s. The poems existed only in manuscript form to be passed round and copied by friends. In 1598 Francis Meres described Shakespeare as 'the most passionate among us to bewail and bemoan the perplexities of love ... witness his sugared sonnets among his private friends'. Some of the later poems may have been written or revised after 1603. In any case, all the sonnets were published (probably without the author's permission) in 1609, with a longer poem called *A lover's complaint*.

The sequence contains 154 sonnets. Each may be read on its own, but together they tell the story of a three-sided love affair between 'I' (the **NARRATOR**, who may or may not be Shakespeare), a 'fair friend' (a handsome young man) and a mysterious 'dark lady'. The poems are probably not about Shakespeare himself, but many scholars have tried to identify the characters and a 'Mr W. H., the only begetter of these ensuing sonnets', who is mentioned on the title page. The following three sonnets combine the **THEMES** of love and time.

Sonnet 18

Shall I compare thee to a summer's day?[1]
Thou art more lovely and more temperate.[2]
Rough winds do shake the darling buds of May,
And summer's lease[3] hath all too short a date.
Sometime too hot the eye of heaven[4] shines,
And often is his gold complexion dimmed;
And every fair from fair sometime declines,
By chance or nature's changing course untrimmed.[5]
But thy eternal summer shall not fade,
Nor lose possession of that fair thou ow'st,[6]
Nor shall Death brag thou wand'rest in his shade,
When in eternal lines[7] to time thou grow'st.
   So long as men can breathe or eyes can see,
   So long lives this, and this gives life to thee.

[1] season [2] constant [3] span of allowed time [4] sun
[5] stripped of decoration [6] the beauty you own
[7] undying verses

How does Shakespeare use the idea of summer in this poem?
How will poetry defeat the changes of time?

Sonnet 73

That time of year thou mayst in me behold[1]
When yellow leaves, or none, or few, do hang
Upon those boughs which shake against the cold,
Bare ruined choirs[2] where late the sweet birds[3] sang.
In me thou seest the twilight of such day
As after sunset fadeth in the west,
Which by and by[4] black night doth take away,
Death's second self,[5] that seals up[6] all in rest.
In me thou seest the glowing of such fire
That on the ashes of his youth doth lie,
As the deathbed whereon[7] it must expire,
Consumed with that which it was nourished by.
   This thou perceiv'st, which makes thy love
                         more strong,
   To love that well which thou must leave[8] ere long.

[1] see [2] ruins of churches [3] choirboys [4] eventually
[5] (sleep) [6] closes (by adding a seal) [7] upon which
[8] give up

The poet compares himself to three things in the three
QUATRAINS. Explain these comparisons.
Which words and details are sad and ominous?
What is the final message of the **COUPLET**?

Sonnet 104

To me, fair friend, you never can be old,
For as you were when first your eye I eyed,
Such seems your beauty still. Three winters cold
Have from the forests shook three summers'
                         pride,[1]
Three beauteous springs to yellow autumn turned
In process[2] of the seasons have I seen,
Three April perfumes in three hot Junes burned,
Since first I saw you fresh, which yet are green.[3]
Ah, yet doth beauty, like a dial hand,[4]
Steal from his figure,[5] and no pace perceived;
So your sweet hue,[6] which methinks[7] still doth
                         stand,
Hath motion, and mine eye may be deceived;
   For fear of which,[8] hear this, thou age unbred:[9]
   Ere you were born was beauty's summer dead.

[1] splendid show of leaves [2] progress [3] youthful
[4] sundial pointer [5] number on a clock face
[6] form (more than colour) [7] I think
[8] to provide against this [9] time to come

*An Elizabethan lover, like Shakespeare's 'fair friend'.
The roses and thorns stand for the delights and pains
of love. A miniature (1588) by Nicholas Hilliard.*

The poet describes three years of a relationship (three
years is the typical span of devotion in sonnet
sequences). What lovingly chosen details are used to
represent those years?
What illusion does the poet have when he looks at the
fair friend? To what is this effect compared?
What concluding message does the sonnet have for
future generations?

W Show how Shakespeare writes about time, love
and poetry in these sonnets.

W Study the **PENTAMETER** line pattern and **RHYME**
scheme of Shakespeare's sonnets. Then try to compose
your own sonnet, based on the theme of time.

D Which is the most impressive of these
Shakespeare sonnets? Think about theme, use of sonnet
shape, comparisons and diction to justify your choice.

4 John Donne (1572-1631): Lover and preacher

Donne's early love poems, *Songs and Sonnets*, probably date from the late 1590s. His TONE is like that of real speech, making the experiences described seem very immediate. His VERSE FORMS are endlessly inventive and he carries the Elizabethan CONCEIT to new heights. The critic Samuel Johnson (1709-1784) looked back with distaste at Donne who, he said, used 'the most heterogeneous ideas yoked by violence together'. He called Donne a 'metaphysical' poet, by which he meant 'too clever'.

After some war service fighting the Spanish, Donne became secretary to Sir Thomas Egerton, an important state official. He secretly married Egerton's niece, Anne More, was dismissed and joked grimly to his wife: 'John Donne: Anne Donne: undone'. Years of hardship followed, although the marriage was happy and produced many children.

Finally, Donne's religious writings impressed King James I. Donne gave up his Catholic faith, entered the Church of England and became Dean of St Paul's Cathedral in London. At this time his wife died. Donne became as passionate a preacher as he had been a poet. In the following passage, the bell mentioned is a funeral bell, heard in the distance:

> No man is an island ... every man is a piece of the continent, a part of the main ... any man's death diminishes me, because I am involved in mankind, and therefore never send to know for whom the bell tolls; it tolls for thee.
>
> (*Devotions*, 1624)

When Donne was near to death, he posed for an artist in his funeral shroud 'with so much sheet turned aside as might show his lean, pale and death-like face'. A statue made from the picture was rescued from the Great Fire of London (1666) and is now in the rebuilt St Paul's Cathedral.

The sun rising

Busy old fool, unruly[1] Sun,
    Why dost thou thus,
Through windows and through curtains[2] call on us?
Must to thy motions lovers' seasons run?
    Saucy pedantic[3] wretch, go chide[4]
    Late school-boys, and our 'prentices,
Go tell court-huntsmen that the King will ride,
Call country ants[5] to harvest offices;
Love, all alike, no season knows, nor clime,[6]
Nor hours, days, months, which are the rags of time.

    Thy beams, so reverend and strong
    Why shouldst thou think?
I could eclipse and cloud them with a wink,
But that I would not lose her sight so long:
    If her eyes have not blinded thine,
    Look, and tomorrow late tell me,
Whether both the Indias of spice and mine[7]
Be where thou left'st them, or lie here with me.
Ask for those kings whom thou saw'st yesterday,
And thou shalt hear, 'All here in one bed lay'.

    She's all States, and all Princes I;
    Nothing else is.
Princes do but play us; compared to this,
All honour's mimic; all wealth alchemy.[8]
    Thou, Sun, art half as happy as we,
    In that the world's contracted thus;
    Thine age asks ease, and since thy duties be
    To warm the world, that's done in warming us.
Shine here to us, and thou art everywhere;
This bed thy centre is, these walls thy sphere.[9]

[1] breaking the rules (of the sun's motion) [2] (on a four-poster bed) [3] insists on keeping time [4] scold [5] farm workers [6] current opinion [7] the Indies, East (famous for spices) and West (close to the gold and silver mines of Central America) [8] worthless material [9] space in which the sun moves

Donne posing in his shroud just before his death. Engraving by Martin Droeshout in Death's Duell *(1632).*

This is an **AUBADE** and an example of wit, or clever argument. The speaker seems to address the sun, but, in fact, much of what he says is a compliment to the woman. The speaker ('I') could be any lover.

Why does the speaker object to the sun shining into the bedroom? What kind of people should it wake? Why do lovers not follow an ordinary time-scheme? How could the speaker avoid seeing the sun? Why will he not do so?
What clever argument is used to show how the sun might work less hard? How do you explain the last line?
Find some sentences and words that show Donne's **COLLOQUIAL STYLE**.
When is the speaker being serious, and when comic and mocking?

A Jacobean beauty: anonymous portrait (around 1610) of Elizabeth Vernon. The women in Donne's love poetry may have looked like this.

Holy Sonnet: Death, be not proud

Donne began writing his sequence of 'holy sonnets' in 1609.

Death, be not proud, though some have callèd thee
   Mighty and dreadful, for thou art not so;
   For those whom thou think'st thou dost
                   overthrow[1]
Die not, poor Death, nor yet canst thou kill me.
From rest and sleep, which but thy pictures be,
   Much pleasure – then, from thee much more
                   must flow;
  And soonest our best men[2] with thee do go,
Rest of their bones and soul's delivery.
Thou'rt slave to fate, chance, kings and
                   desperate men,
  And dost with poison, war, and sickness dwell;
  And poppy[3] or charms[4] can make us sleep as well,
And better than thy stroke.[5] Why swell'st thou[6] then?
  One short sleep past, we wake eternally,
  And death shall be no more. Death, thou
                  shalt die.

[1] kill   [2] people who die young and are therefore less damaged by sin   [3] opium   [4] spells, or perhaps hypnosis [5] blow   [6] do you puff yourself up

The poem is like a short sermon, which starts with contemplation of a *memento mori* ('a reminder of death'), which was usually an actual or pictured skull. This forced the onlooker to consider death and God's judgement.

Why is death too proud of its powers?
The second **QUATRAIN** gives two more reasons for not fearing death. Explain them.
In the third quatrain, death is pitied for the work it does and the company it keeps. What are these?
The final **COUPLET** gives us the text from the Bible on which this poem-sermon is based:

The trumpet shall sound, and the dead shall be raised incorruptible ... O death, where is thy sting? O grave, where is thy victory?
                   (1 Corinthians 15:52-55)

What is Donne's final message?

W Choose one of the poems and show how Donne deals with love or death. Follow the clever arguments and conceits clearly.

D Discuss the strange comparisons that Donne uses. Which do you think work best? Do you think they are impressive, or just too clever?

•PART 2•

Voices from the seventeenth century

5 Robert Herrick (1591-1674): Seizing the day

When he was young, Herrick was apprenticed to a London jeweller: later, he wrote jewel-like poems, 1,400 of which appeared in his only book, *Hesperides* (1648). Herrick avoided the complex, **'CONCEITED' STYLE** of Donne, preferring the plain, concise manner of Ben Jonson (1572-1637).

Frontispiece of Herrick's collected poems (1648), published when he was briefly dismissed from his Devon living by Cromwell's government.

In 1629 Herrick became vicar of Dean Prior in Devon, where he remained for the rest of his life, except when he was briefly expelled by the Puritans during the Civil War. He lived in an eccentric, bachelor style: a domesticated pig, that could drink from a tankard, roamed freely in his rooms.

If he sometimes found 'dull Devonshire' tiresome and missed London society, it had its consolations, such as the beauty of the countryside and its rich traditions, like May Day or Harvest Home. Herrick wrote poems about these festivals and also about 'many dainty Mistresses' – Julia, Anthea, Dianeme – who may be real or imagined. The women are pictured with exquisite skill, but there is often a dark undercurrent to the poems.

To Dianeme

Sweet, be not proud of those two eyes
Which starlike sparkle in their skies;
Nor be you proud that you can see
All hearts your captives,[1] yours yet free;
Be you not proud of that rich hair
Which wantons[2] with the love-sick air;
Whenas[3] that ruby which you wear,
Sunk from the tip of your soft ear,
Will last to be a precious stone
When all your world of beauty's gone.

[1] prisoners   [2] flirts   [3] whereas

What are the particular beauties of the woman? Which words and comparisons suggest these best?
How do men react to her?
How is the ruby used as a warning against vanity?

Herrick borrowed **THEMES** from Latin and Greek poets. The Roman writer Horace used the key **PHRASE** *carpe diem* ('seize the day'). The idea was much copied by poets of the 17th century, when the average life was so brief.

To the virgins, to make much of time

Gather ye[1] rosebuds while ye may,
  Old Time is still a-flying:
And this same flower that smiles to-day
  To-morrow will be dying.

The glorious lamp of heaven, the sun,
  The higher he's a-getting,
The sooner will his race be run,
  And nearer he's to setting.

That age is best which is the first,
  When youth and blood are warmer;
But being spent, the worse, and worst
  Times still succeed the former.

Then be not coy,[2] but use your time,
  And while ye may, go marry:
For having lost but once your prime,[3]
  You may for ever tarry.[4]

[1] you must gather [2] shy [3] youth [4] wait (for a husband, or for death)

What are the girls compared to in the first verse?
What comparison is used for time in the second verse?
'That age' is a reference to the mythical Golden Age, when people lived in perfect happiness, and then declined. How does that idea fit with youth?
Which verse is most impressive?

Anne Finch, Countess of Winchelsea (1661-1720), was a leading woman poet of the 17th century. She wrote a good-humoured but sarcastic reply to Herrick.

The unequal fetters

Could we stop the time that's flying
  Or recall it when 'tis past,
Put far off the day of dying
  Or make youth for ever last,
To love would then be worth our cost.

But since we must lose those graces
  Which at first your hearts have won
And you seek for in new faces
  When our spring of life is done,
It would but urge our ruin on.

Free as Nature's first intention
  Was to make us, I'll be found,
Nor by subtle Man's invention
  Yield to be in fetters bound
By one that walks a freer round.[1]

Marriage does but slightly tie men
  Whilst close prisoners we remain,
They the larger slaves of Hymen[2]
  Still are begging love again
At the full length of all their chain.

[1] enjoys a less restricted lifestyle [2] the god of marriage

Why is time unfair to women?
What exactly does the poet object to about marriage?
What was 'Nature's first intention' to women?
How are the ideas of chains and fetters used for each sex?

W Compare the ideas and styles of the two poems above.

D Discuss Herrick's message in *To the virgins* and Anne Finch's answer.

Flowers were, to Herrick, the perfect **SYMBOL** of the fragile beauty of the world.

To daffodils

Fair daffodils, we weep to see
  You haste away so soon;
As yet the early-rising sun
  Has not attained his noon.
    Stay, stay
    Until the hasting day
      Has run
    But to the evensong;[1]
And, having prayed together, we
  Will go with you along.

We have short time to stay as you,
  We have as short a spring;
As quick a growth to meet decay,
  As you, or anything.
    We die
    As your hours do, and dry
      Away
    Like to the summer's rain;
Or as the pearls of morning's dew,
  Ne'er to be found again.

[1] evening church service

Herrick realises that this year's daffodils are withering at the end of their brief season. What conclusions does he draw from them about human life?
Do you like the very short lines? Which are most effective?

W Compare this poem with Wordsworth's daffodil poem (page 38).

6 George Herbert (1593-1633): Poems from *The Temple*

Herbert came from an important noble family: his two brothers were prominent at court. Although he was successful at Cambridge University, he turned away from public life. Eventually he became rector of Bemerton in Wiltshire; he was 'like a saint, unspotted of the world, full of alms deeds, full of humility'.

His mother was a patron of John Donne, whose poems Herbert probably imitated. However, Herbert destroyed all his non-religious verse and wrote the 160 poems collected as *The Temple*, published after his death. It was intended for private circulation but became a best seller. The poems present 'a picture of the many spiritual conflicts that have passed between God and my soul'.

Virtue

Sweet day, so cool, so calm, so bright,
The bridal[1] of the earth and sky:
The dew shall weep thy fall tonight,
    For thou must die.

Sweet rose, whose hue[2] angry and brave
Bids the rash gazer wipe his eye:
Thy root is ever in its grave,
    And thou must die.

Sweet spring, full of sweet days and roses,
A box where sweets compacted[3] lie:
My music shows ye have your closes,[4]
    And all must die.

Only a sweet and virtuous soul,
Like seasoned timber never gives;
But though the whole world turn to coal,
    Then chiefly lives.

[1] marriage   [2] colour   [3] closely packed together
[4] ends (of passages of music)

Herbert in his garden at Bemerton, Wiltshire. Painting (1855) by William Dyce .

Herbert meditates on the brief existence of beautiful things, a popular 17th-century **THEME**.

The first **IMAGE** is a lovely day. Why is this a 'bridal' of earth and sky? What does the fall of dew express? The second image is a perfect rose. How does its colour affect the onlooker? Why is the root 'in its grave'? The third image is spring. What fantastic comparison is used here? How do the 'closes' fit in with spring? What does survive time? To what is it compared? How does Herbert use the **REFRAIN** in the last verse?

Redemption

Having been tenant long to a rich Lord,
    Not thriving, I resolvèd to be bold,
And make a suit[1] unto him, to afford
    A new small-rented lease, and cancel the old.
In heaven at his manor I him sought:
    They told me there that he was lately gone
About some land, which he had dearly bought
    Long since on earth, to take possession.
I straight returned, and knowing his great birth,
    Sought him accordingly in great resorts:
    In cities, theatres, gardens, parks, and courts.
At length I heard a ragged noise and mirth
    Of thieves and murderers: there I him
                    espied,[2]
    Who straight, *Your suit is granted*, said, and
                    died.

[1] ask for favour   [2] caught sight of

This **SONNET** is also a **PARABLE**. The poet sees himself as a tenant who rents his estate (his condition of life on earth) from a wealthy lord (Christ). He wants to change the terms of his lease and move to a smaller property. The larger estate may represent Herbert's first ambition for a state career; the smaller, either his more humble church post, or his wish for a simpler style of life and faith.

Where does Herbert go to look for Christ? Christ has returned to earth in a second coming to take over the Christian world 'so dearly bought'. To what does this **PHRASE** refer? Where does the poet find Christ? Where was Christ seen with 'thieves and murderers' previously (think of the crucifixion story)? What is Christ's fate again? What is the point of this parable?

Love

Love bade me welcome; yet my soul drew back,
        Guilty of dust[1] and sin.[2]
But quick-eyed Love, observing me grow slack[3]
        From my first entrance in,
Drew nearer to me, sweetly questioning,
        If I lacked anything.

'A guest', I answered, 'worthy to be here.'
        Love said, 'You shall be he.'
'I, the unkind, ungrateful? Ah, my dear,
        I cannot look on thee.'
Love took my hand, and smiling did reply,
        'Who made the eyes but I?'[4]

'Truth, Lord, but I have marred[5] them; let my shame
        Go where it doth deserve.'
'And know you not', says Love, 'who bore the blame?'
        'My dear, then I will serve.'
'You must sit down', says Love, 'and taste my meat.'[6]
        So I did sit and eat.[7]

[1] (Adam was made from earth)   [2] (man inherits Adam's sin)   [3] slow down   [4] God created man   [5] spoilt (i.e. stopped my eyes from seeing Christ)   [6] (body and blood of Christ celebrated at Communion)   [7] fully accept faith in God

The ideas of Love (Christ) and food relate to communion and to parables in the Bible. Matthew 22:14, for example, compares heaven to a wedding feast where 'many are called, but few are chosen', and Revelation 19:9 says 'happy are those who are invited to the wedding supper of the Lamb'.

Which words and phrases describe the kindness of Christ? Which words describe Herbert's feeling of inadequacy? Where is the very simple **STYLE** most impressive? How effective is the use of conversation?

D Which of these poems gives the best picture of religious faith? Support your answer by looking at diction, comparison and themes.

W How does Herbert write about religious doubts and faith in these poems?

W Herbert produced some shape poems, such as *Easter wings* (see below), where the words and lines are placed to form a shape. Try composing your own shape poem, not necessarily on a religious theme.

The Church.

¶ *Easter wings.*

My tender age in sorrow did beginne
And still with sicknesse and shame
Thou didst so punish sinne,
That I became
Most thinne.
With thee
Let me combine,
And feel this day thy victorie:
For, if I imp my wing on thine,
Affliction shall advance the flight in me.

The Church.

¶ *Easter wings.*

Lord, who createdst man in wealth and stor
Though foolishly he lost the same,
Decaying more and more,
Till he became
Most poore:
With thee
O let me rise
As larks, harmoniously,
And sing this day thy victories:
Then shall the fall further the flight in

Easter wings: *a pattern poem in the shape of two sets of angel's wings.*

7 John Milton (1608-1674): Fame is the spur

Milton sensed his poetic vocation early and wrote his first outstanding poem, *Christ's nativity*, in 1629, when he was still at Cambridge University. His distaste for the Church of England made him give up his plan to enter it, and he withdrew to his wealthy father's house to follow an ambitious study programme.

When Edward King, a Cambridge friend, was drowned at sea, Milton wrote an **ELEGY**, *Lycidas*

(1637), for him. It is not just about death – Milton also discusses the poet's role and ambition:

Fame is the spur that the clear spirit doth raise
To scorn delights and live laborious days.

After travelling in Italy, Milton wrote pamphlets as the English Civil War approached in the 1640s. He supported Parliament against the Royalists, argued for a free press in *Areopagitica* (1644), and defended the execution of Charles I (1649). He was rewarded with a high official post in the Cromwell government, but by 1652 he had gone blind, a horror movingly described in his last verse play, *Samson Agonistes* (1671):

> O dark, dark, dark, amid the blaze of noon
> Irrecoverably dark, total eclipse
> Without all hope of day ...

At the Restoration of Charles II in 1660, Milton's books were publicly burned. He was imprisoned and nearly executed. In retirement in London, he dictated his **EPIC POEM,** *Paradise lost* (1667), the story of the Fall of Man. In the following section, Adam and Eve are expelled from the Garden of Eden:

> They, looking back, all the eastern side beheld
> Of Paradise, so late[1] their happy seat,[2]
> Waved over by that flaming brand,[3] the gate
> With dreadful faces thronged[4] and fiery arms.
> Some natural tears they dropped, but wiped
> them soon;
> The world was all before them, where to choose
> Their place of rest, and Providence[5] their guide:
> They hand in hand, with wandering steps and
> slow,
> Through Eden took their solitary way.
>
> (*Paradise lost*, Book 12)

[1] recently [2] home [3] sword [4] crowded [5] God

He also completed a sequel, *Paradise regained* (1671).

Milton wrote his contrasting twin poems *L'Allegro* ('the lively man') and *Il Penseroso* ('the thoughtful man') while he was still at Cambridge. The poems use apparently simple **OCTOSYLLABIC COUPLETS,** and contain vivid little pictures.

from: Il Penseroso

> Thee, chantress,[1] oft the woods among
> I woo[2] to hear thy evensong,[3]
> And, missing thee, I walk unseen
> On the dry, smooth-shaven green
> To behold the wandering moon
> Riding near her highest noon,
> Like one that had been led astray
> Through the heaven's wide pathless way
> And oft,[4] as if her head she bowed,
> Stooping through a fleecy cloud.
> Oft on a plat[5] of rising ground,
> I hear the far-off curfew sound
> Over some wide-watered shore,
> Swinging slow with sullen roar;
> Or, if the air will not permit,
> Some still removèd place will fit,

The bellman *(1874) by Samuel Palmer, based on* Il Penseroso.

> Where glowing embers through the room
> Teach light to counterfeit a gloom,
> Far from all resort of mirth,
> Save the cricket on the hearth
> Or the bellman's[6] drowsy charm
> To bless the doors from nightly harm,
> Or let my lamp at midnight hour
> Be seen in some high, lonely tower.
> ...
> And when the sun begins to fling
> His flaring beams, me, goddess,[7] bring
> To archèd walks of twilight groves
> And shadows brown that Sylvan[8] loves,
> Of pine or monumental oak
> Where the rude[9] axe with heavèd stroke
> Was never heard the nymphs to daunt
> Or fright them from their hallowed haunt.
> There in close covert[10] by some brook,
> Where no profaner[11] eye may look,
> Hide me from day's garish eye,[12]
> While the bee, with honied thigh,
> That at her flowery work doth sing,
> And the waters murmuring
> With such consort as they keep,
> Entice the dewy-feathered sleep

[1] nightingale [2] seek [3] evening service [4] often [5] area
[6] (nightwatchman who rings the time with his bell)
[7] spirit of melancholy [8] Sylvanus, god of the woods
[9] rough [10] dense forest [11] more scornful of sacred
things [12] the sun

What various places and experiences does Il Penseroso enjoy here? Which do you think are most impressive?

W Compose your own piece, in prose or poetry, about the quiet pleasures and moods you enjoy, such as favourite places, times of day, reading ...

from: *L'Allegro*

To hear the lark begin his flight
And, singing, startle the dull night
From his watch-tower in the skies
Till the dappled dawn doth rise;
Then to come in spite of sorrow[1]
And at my window bid good-morrow
Through the sweet-briar or the vine
Or the twisted eglantine,[2]
While the cock with lively din
Scatters the rear of darkness thin,
And to the stack or the barn door
Stoutly[3] struts his dames before,
Oft listening how the hounds and horn
Cheerly rouse the slumbering morn,
From the side of some hoar[4] hill
Through the high wood echoing shrill.
Sometime walking[5] not unseen
By hedgerow elms on hillocks green,
Right against the eastern gate
Where the great sun begins his state,
Robed in flames and amber light,
The clouds in thousand liveries dight,[6]
While the ploughman near at hand
Whistles o'er the furrowed land,
And the milkmaid singeth blithe,[7]
And the mower whets[8] his scythe,
And every shepherd tells his tale[9]
Under the hawthorn in the dale.[10]
Straight mine eye hath caught new pleasures
Whilst the landscape round it measures

Russet lawns and fallows grey
Where the nibbling flocks do stray,
Mountains on whose barren breast
The labouring clouds do often rest,
Meadows trim with daisies pied,[11]
Shallow brooks and rivers wide.

[1] the lark comes to chase away any sadness in L'Allegro
[2] honeysuckle   [3] bravely   [4] grey   [5] (L'Allegro leaves his cottage)   [6] dressed in colourful clothes   [7] happily
[8] sharpens   [9] counts sheep   [10] valley   [11] having different colours in different parts

W   You are L'Allegro. You wake in his cottage. Describe the sounds you hear at dawn and what you see around you as you walk in the countryside.

D   What do you enjoy about life and the world around you in a cheerful or thoughtful mood?

Sonnet: *Methought I saw my late espousèd saint*

Methought I saw my late[1] espousèd saint
  Brought to me like Alcestis[2] from the grave,
  Whom Jove's great son[3] to her glad husband
                                           gave,
  Rescued from death by force, though pale and
                                           faint.
Mine, as whom washed from spot of childbed
                                           taint
  Purification in the old Law[4] did save,
  And such as yet once more I trust to have
  Full sight of her in heaven without restraint,
Came vested[5] all in white, pure as her mind.
  Her face was veiled, yet to my fancied[6] sight
  Love, sweetness, goodness, in her person
                                           shined
So clear as in no face with more delight.
  But O as to embrace me she inclined,[7]
  I waked, she fled, and day brought back my
                                           night.

[1] dead   [2] woman who returned from death in Greek legend   [3] Hercules, who brought Alcestis back from the underworld   [4] Jewish law required 66 days to 'purify' a woman after childbirth   [5] dressed   [6] imagined   [7] leaned

Milton married three times. This **SONNET** probably refers to his second wife, Katherine.

Look up the Greek stories of Hercules rescuing Alcestis, and of Orpheus rescuing Eurydice. How do they help you to understand the poem?
How does Milton's wife look in his dream?
What qualities does he see in her face under the veil?
What happened as she stooped to kiss him?
What does 'day brought back my night' mean?

W   When Milton wakes he scribbles down the story of his sad dream. What does he write?

Sir Thomas Aston at the death-bed of his first wife *(around 1650) by John Souch. Milton lost two wives in childbirth.*

8 Andrew Marvell (1621-1678): Girls and gardens

Marvell was born in Hull and his first education was 'among boatswains and cabin boys'. After studying Latin and Greek at Cambridge University, he travelled in Europe, perhaps to escape the English Civil War. In 1650 he became tutor to the daughter of Lord Fairfax, a Parliamentary general who, having opposed the execution of Charles I in 1649, retired to his Yorkshire estate.

In 1657 Marvell moved to London to become John Milton's assistant in Cromwell's government. Marvell survived the Restoration of Charles II in 1660 and remained Member of Parliament for Hull until his death, despite writing SATIRICAL poems attacking the government.

His collected poems were published only after his death. He wrote some political pieces, like his *Horatian ODE on Cromwell*, in which he describes Charles I's courage in facing execution:

> He nothing common did or mean
> Upon that memorable scene,
>   But with his keener eye
>   The axe's edge did try.

Marvell's poems typically contain complex thoughts about life, time and love. He seemed to write them for his own amusement, even translating their elaborate CONCEITS into Latin.

The picture of little T.C.[1] in a prospect[2] of flowers

'Green' is one of Marvell's favourite words. It describes the green of the lawn, but also suggests hope, with which the word is associated in Christian thinking.

>   See with what simplicity
> This nymph[3] begins her golden days!
>   In the green grass she loves to lie,
> And there with her fair aspect[4] tames
> The wilder flowers, and gives them names;
>   But only with the roses plays,
>   And them does tell
> What colour best becomes them, and what smell.

>   Who can foretell for what high cause
> This darling of the gods was born?
>   Yet this is she whose chaster laws
> The wanton Love[5] shall one day fear,
> And, under her command severe,
>   See his bow broke and ensigns[6] torn.
>   Happy who can
> Appease[7] this virtuous enemy of man!

>   O then let me in time compound[8]
> And parley[9] with those conquering eyes,
>   Ere[10] they have tried their force to wound;
> Ere with their glancing wheels they drive
> In triumph over hearts that strive,
>   And them that yield but more despise:
>   Let me be laid,[11]
> Where I may see thy glories from some shade.

>   Meantime, whilst every verdant[12] thing
> Itself does at thy beauty charm,
>   Reform the errors of the Spring;
> Make that the tulips may have share
> Of sweetness,[13] seeing they are fair,
>   And roses of their thorns disarm;
>   But most procure[14]
> That violets may a longer age endure.

>   But O, young beauty of the woods,
> Whom Nature courts with fruits and flowers,
>   Gather the flowers, but spare the buds;
> Lest Flora,[15] angry at thy crime
> To kill her infants in their prime,
>   Do quickly make the example yours;
>   And ere we see,
> Nip in the blossom all our hopes and thee.

[1] possibly an actual girl called Theophila Cornewall [2] extensive view [3] girl [4] face [5] Cupid [6] banners or flags (young man's injured pride) [7] calm [8] come to an agreement with [9] discuss the terms of peace (with an enemy) [10] before [11] buried [12] green [13] scent [14] arrange [15] the goddess of flowers

In the first verse, the poet describes the girl. What are her 'golden days'?
Eve supposedly gave the flowers their names in Eden. How does the girl in the poem play with the flowers? How does the poet think that T. C. will behave when she grows up? Why will Cupid have his bow broken? Marvell describes her harsh treatment of men in future time in terms of warfare. Which words and PHRASES suggest this in the second and third verses?
In the fourth verse T. C.'s power over the flowers is considered. What changes will she make to them? Marvell expresses genuine fear in the last verse: another Theophila Cornewall, elder sister to this one, had died in infancy, which may explain the last line. What do the buds stand for? What will happen to T. C. if she picks them?

W What pictures and ideas come to Marvell as he watches T. C. in the garden?

A young woman of the Civil War era: miniature (around 1660) by Samuel Cooper .

To his coy mistress

Had we but world enough, and time,
This coyness,[1] Lady, were no crime.
We would sit down and think which way
To walk and pass our long love's day.
Thou by the Indian Ganges'[2] side
Shouldst rubies find: I by the tide
Of Humber[3] would complain.[4] I would
Love you ten years before the Flood,[5]
And you should, if you please, refuse
Till the conversion of the Jews.[6]
My vegetable[7] love should grow
Vaster than empires, and more slow;
An hundred years should go to praise
Thine eyes and on thy forehead gaze;
Two hundred to adore each breast;
But thirty thousand to the rest;
An age at least to every part,
And the last age should show your heart;
For, Lady, you deserve this state,
Nor would I love at lower rate.
   But at my back I always hear
Time's wingèd chariot hurrying near;
And yonder[8] all before us lie
Deserts of vast eternity.

Thy beauty shall no more be found,
Nor, in thy marble vault,[9] shall sound
My echoing song: then worms shall try
That long preserved virginity,
And your quaint[10] honour turn to dust,
And into ashes all my lust:
The grave's a fine and private place,
But none, I think, do there embrace.
   Now therefore, while the youthful hue[11]
Sits on thy skin like morning dew,
And while thy willing soul transpires[12]
At every pore with instant fires,
Now let us sport us[13] while we may,
And now, like amorous birds of prey,
Rather at once our time devour
Than languish in his slow-chapt[14] power.
Let us roll all our strength and all
Our sweetness up into one ball,
And tear our pleasures with rough strife
Thorough the iron gates of life:
Thus, though we cannot make our sun
Stand still, yet we will make him run.

[1] shyness [2] sacred river of India
[3] river in Marvell's native Hull [4] bemoan my love
[5] Noah's flood [6] end of time [7] growing [8] over there
[9] tomb [10] over-scrupulous [11] colour
[12] breathes out through the skin
[13] enjoy ourselves in loving [14] slowly devouring

This is Marvell's most famous poem, on the *carpe diem* ('seize the day') idea borrowed from the Roman poet, Horace. He urges his mistress to surrender to him before she loses her beauty and time destroys them both. The **RHYMING TETRAMETERS** underline the urgency of his arguments.

How does Marvell pretend to feel about time in the first 20 lines?
What would the lovers do if they lived in a timeless universe?
How does the poet use **HYPERBOLE** sarcastically?
How does the mood change in the second section?
Which phrase vividly describes time?
What terrifying pictures of death are given?
What dry joke does the poet make about the grave?
The last section starts with the urgent time word, 'Now'. How is the woman described here?
What are the 'iron gates of life'?
What do the last two lines mean?

W Compare this poem and its images and arguments with Herrick's *To the virgins* and Anne Finch's reply (both on page 16).

D What reasons might the 'coy mistress' have for turning down Marvell?

9 Henry Vaughan (?1622-1695): The sparkling flint

Vaughan was born and lived most of his life in a house overlooking the River Usk, near Brecon in Wales. He and his twin, Thomas, were brought up speaking Welsh. This influenced his poems, notably in the use of his favourite word 'white', which means 'fair, blessed or happy' in Welsh.

The Civil War stopped his plans to be a lawyer. Both brothers fought on the Royalist side. Then Henry returned to the 'primrosed fields' of his home to be a doctor.

Inspired by George Herbert, Vaughan wrote poems, and published *Olor Iscanus* ('The swan of Usk') in 1647, and *Silex scintillans* ('The sparkling flint') in 1650. Vaughan never wrote so well again, instead dabbling in alchemy and planning a book on shooting stars. No portrait of him survives.

The title page of Vaughan's collection Silex scintillans *(1650). God's angry bolts are striking Vaughan's hard, flinty heart to produce tears, which are the poems.*

Happy that first white age

Happy that first white age! when we
Lived by the Earth's mere charity:
No soft luxurious diet then
Had effeminated men,[1]
No other meat[2] nor wine had any
Than the coarse mast[3] or simple honey,
And by the parents' care laid up
Cheap berries did the children sup.
No pompous wear was in those days,
Of gummy[4] silks or scarlet bays;[5]
Their beds were on some flowery brink[6]
And clear spring-water was their drink.
The shady pine in the sun's heat
Was their cool and known retreat;
For then 'twas not cut down, but stood
The youth and glory of the wood.
The daring sailor with his slaves
Then had not cut the swelling waves,
Nor for desire of foreign store[7]
Seen any but his native shore.
No stirring drum had scarred that age,
Nor the shrill trumpet's active rage:
No wounds by bitter hatred made
With warm blood soiled the shining blade;
For how could hostile madness arm
An age of love to public harm?
When common justice none withstood,
Nor sought rewards for spilling blood.
    Oh that at length our age would raise
Into the temper[8] of those days!
But (worse then Aetna's[9] fires!) debate[10]
And avarice[11] inflame our state.
Alas! who was it that first found
Gold hid of purpose[12] under ground;
That sought out pearls, and dived to find
Such precious perils for mankind!

[1] made men lose their strength [2] food [3] nuts [4] sticky
[5] badges of office [6] edge of a river [7] wealth [8] frame of
mind [9] (a volcano) [10] argument [11] greed
[12] deliberately

Vaughan has adapted his translation of a Latin passage by a Roman writer, Boethius, to fit his own anxieties about the Civil War.

What qualities did the 'first white age' have? What, by contrast, are the evils and weaknesses of the modern world?
How is war described?
Where did man first go wrong?

[W] Compose your own brief picture of human life in an ideal age.

Spring

In March birds couple, a new birth
Of herbs and flowers breaks through the earth,
But in the grave none stirs his head;
Long is th' Impris'ment of the dead.

This poem is a translation of work by the 6th-century Welsh poet, Anerrin.

How are life and death described and contrasted? Why is it strange that a religious thinker such as Vaughan should like these lines?

The retreat

Happy those early days! when I
Shined in my angel-infancy.
Before I understood this place
Appointed for my second race,[1]
Or taught my soul to fancy aught[2]
But a white, celestial[3] thought;
When yet I had not walked above
A mile or two from my first love,
And looking back (at that short space)
Could see a glimpse of his bright face;
When on some gilded[4] cloud or flower
My gazing soul would dwell an hour,
And in those weaker glories spy[5]
Some shadows of eternity;
Before I taught my tongue to wound
My conscience with a sinful sound,
Or had the black art to dispense
A several[6] sin to every sense,
But felt through all this fleshly dress
Bright shoots of everlastingness.
   Oh how I long to travel back
And tread again that ancient track!
That I might once more reach that plain
Where first I left my glorious train,[7]
From whence the enlightened spirit sees
That shady city of palm trees;
But (ah!) my soul with too much stay[8]
Is drunk, and staggers in the way.
Some men a forward motion love,
But I by backward steps would move,
And, when this dust falls to the urn,[9]
In that state I came, return.

[1] (the poet's life on earth – his first was in heaven)
[2] imagine anything [3] heavenly [4] covered with gold
[5] see [6] different [7] series of experiences
[8] time on earth [9] when I die

The poem is like a sermon, based on the Biblical text: 'Whoever does not accept the Kingdom of God like a child will never enter it' (Mark 10:15).

What does Vaughan look back to in childhood?
Why did the poet admire flowers or clouds?
How did Vaughan change as he grew up?
What are 'bright shoots of everlastingness'?
What is 'the city of palm trees'?
How does Vaughan contrast himself with other people?
What is the poet's final wish?

Vaughan was influenced by the emblem books of the early 17th century. Each emblem has a motto, picture and short verse.

D   Look at the picture below. What might the emblem shown mean? Try to explain all the details.

W   Write your own motto and draw your own emblem about life and its problems.

Emblem books, which offered religious messages in words and pictures, were enormously popular in the 17th century. This is from George Wither's Collection of Emblemes *(1635). Vaughan often imitated the emblem idea in his poems.*

•PART 3•
The Augustans and the eighteenth century

10 John Dryden (1631-1700): The full resounding line

Dryden started work as a clerk in Oliver Cromwell's government. After the Restoration of Charles II in 1660, Dryden decided to write. His plays for the newly reopened theatres were successful, especially *All for Love*, based on Shakespeare's *Antony and Cleopatra*. His poems praising the new King and attacking his enemies were so effective that he was made **POET LAUREATE**.

In his **SATIRES**, Dryden used the **HEROIC COUPLET**. Alexander Pope, who later used the form, praised Dryden as creator of 'The varying verse, the full resounding line' (from: *Satires: To Augustus*, 1733). Dryden used the balance and **RHYMING** sting of the couplet to savage politicians and a rival poet, Thomas Shadwell:

> The midwife laid her hand on his thick skull,
> With this prophetic blessing – Be thou dull ...
>
> (from: *MacFlecknoe*, 1684)

The mid-1660s were dark times for London. The plague killed thousands in 1665 and in 1666 a huge fire destroyed most of the city. Dryden had left London to escape the plague and so missed the fire. When he returned, he wrote *Annus mirabilis* (Latin for 'the wonderful year'), concentrating on Charles II's sea victory against the Dutch, and the Great Fire.

from: Annus mirabilis: The Great Fire of London

> The diligence of trades and noiseful gain,[1]
>   And luxury,[2] more late, asleep were laid:
> All was the Night's, and in her silent reign
>   No sound the rest of nature did invade.

In this deep quiet, from what source unknown,
  Those seeds of fire their fatal birth disclose;
And first, few scatt'ring sparks about were blown,
  Big with the flames that to our ruin rose.

Then, in some close-pent[3] room it crept along,
  And, smould'ring as it went, in silence fed;
Till th' infant monster, with devouring strong,
  Walk'd boldly upright with exalted head.

Now, like some rich or mighty murderer,
  Too great for prison, which he breaks with gold;
Who fresher for new mischiefs does appear,
  And dares the world to tax[4] him with the old;

So scapes th' insulting fire his narrow jail,
  And makes small outlets into open air;
There the fierce winds his tender force assail,[5]
  And beat him downward to his first repair.[6]

The winds, like crafty courtesans, withheld[7]
  His flames from burning, but to blow them more:
And, every fresh attempt, he is repell'd
  With faint denials, weaker than before.

And now, no longer letted[8] of his prey,
  He leaps up at it with inrag'd[9] desire;
O'erlooks the neighbours with a wide survey,[10]
  And nods at every house his threat'ning fire.

[1] busy working people [2] party-goers [3] confined
[4] accuse [5] attack his still weak flames [6] home
[7] stopped [8] deprived [9] angry [10] look around

How does the fire grow?
Look at these key words and explain what is compared to what: 'seeds'; 'sparks'; 'big with the flames'; 'infant monster'; 'mighty murderer'; 'scapes ... his narrow jail'; 'nods'.

The Great Fire of London (1666). The diarist Samuel Pepys 'saw the fire grow ... in a most horrid, malicious bloody flame ... it made me weep to see it. The churches and houses and all on fire and flaming at once ...' (Diary, 2 September 1666).

The ghosts of traitors from the Bridge¹ descend,
    With bold-fanatic spectres to rejoice;
About the fire into a dance they bend,
    And sing their sabbath notes² with feeble voice.

Our guardian angel saw them where he sate
    Above the palace of our slumb'ring king;
He sigh'd, abandoning his charge to fate,
    And, drooping, oft look'd back upon the wing.

¹ (the heads of those who had been executed, which were then placed on the gate of London Bridge)
² songs sung at witches' covens

What do the ghosts and the guardian angel of the city seem to do ?

At length the crackling noise and dreadful blaze
    Call'd up some waking lover to the sight;
And long it was ere he the rest could raise,
    Whose heavy eyelids yet were full of night.

The next¹ to danger, hot pursued by fate,
    Half-cloth'd, half-naked, hastily retire;
And frighted mothers strike their breasts, too late,
    For helpless infants left amidst² the fire.

Their cries soon waken all the dwellers near;
    Now murmuring noises rise in every street;
The more remote run stumbling with their fear,
    And in the dark men justle³ as they meet.

¹ nearest   ² in the middle of   ³ bump into each other

What details does Dryden use to describe the growing panic? Which are most effective?

So weary bees in little cells repose;¹
    But if night-robbers lift the well-stor'd hive,
An humming thro' their waxen city grows,
    And out upon each other's wings they drive.²

Now streets grow throng'd³ and busy as by day:
    Some run for buckets to the hallow'd choir:⁴
Some cut the pipes⁵ and some the engines play;⁶
    And some more bold mount⁷ ladders to the fire.

In vain; for from the East a Belgian wind
    His hostile breath thro' the dry rafters sent;
The flames impell'd⁸ soon left their foes behind,
    And forward with a nton fury went.

A key⁹ of fire ran all along the shore,
    And lighten'd all the river with a blaze;
The waken'd tides began again to roar,
    And wond'ring fish in shining waters gaze.

¹ rest   ² push   ³ crowded   ⁴ (fire buckets were kept in churches)   ⁵ (wooden water pipes were cut in emergencies)   ⁶ spray with hoses from fire engines
⁷ climb   ⁸ forced on   ⁹ line

To what are the city's refugees compared?
Who are east wind's 'foes' ('enemies')?
How is the viewpoint changed in the last verse?

W After more research, write your own poem or diary description of the Great Fire, perhaps including some of the details given here.

D Interview various survivors about what they saw during the Great Fire of London, using details given in the poem.

11 Alexander Pope (1688-1744): Satire and true wit

When he was 12, infected milk gave Pope a spinal illness that deformed his body and began what he called 'this long disease, my life'. As an adult, Pope was only 1.37 m tall.

Pope's wealthy father encouraged him to write. His father's rich, cultivated friends introduced him to the London coffee houses, where writers and politicians met. Here Pope saw Dryden as an old man and entered the savage battleground of writers. Pope himself was described as a 'downright monkey' and a 'hunch-backed toad' by a pompous critic whom he had offended, but he had his revenge in *The Dunciad* (1728), an attack on hack authors.

Pope's verse translations of the Greek poems *The Iliad* and *The Odyssey* gave him enough money to buy a house at Twickenham. There he produced his greatest poems, which often imitated the Latin **SATIRES** and **EPISTLES** of his favourite Roman poets, Juvenal and Horace. He wrote almost all his verse in **HEROIC COUPLETS**, often using **ANTITHESIS**, for example, in his attack on the writer Joseph Addison (1672-1719), who could:

> Damn with faint praise, assent with civil leer,
> And, without sneering, teach the rest to sneer.
> Willing to wound, and yet afraid to strike,
> Just hint a fault, and hesitate dislike.

Pope never married, but had close friendships with women, including Teresa and Martha Blount. When Martha caught smallpox in 1714, they both had to leave London during the exitement of George I's coronation. Pope wrote Martha a poem-letter, teasing her about the dullness of country life. He calls her 'Zephalinda'.

Epistle to Miss Blount on her leaving the town, after the coronation

As some fond[1] virgin, whom her mother's care
Drags from the town to wholesome country air,
Just when she learns to roll a melting eye,
And hear a spark,[2] yet think no danger nigh;[3]
From the dear man unwilling she must sever,[4]
Yet takes one kiss before she parts for ever:
Thus from the world fair Zephalinda flew,
Saw others happy, and with sighs withdrew;
Not that their pleasures caused her discontent,
She sighed not that they stayed, but that she went.
   She went to plain-work,[5] and to purling[6] brooks,
Old-fashioned halls, dull aunts, and croaking rooks:

She went from opera, park, assembly, play,
To morning walks, and prayers three hours a-day;
To pass her time 'twixt[7] reading and bohea,[8]
To muse,[9] and spill her solitary tea,
Or o'er cold coffee trifle with the spoon,
Count the slow clock, and dine exact at noon;
Divert her eyes with pictures in the fire,
Hum half a tune, tell stories to the squire;
Up to her godly garret[10] after seven,
There starve and pray, for that's the way to Heaven.
   Some squire, perhaps, you take delight to rack;[11]
Whose game is whisk,[12] whose treat a toast in sack;[13]
Who visits with a gun, present you birds,
Then gives a smacking buss[14] and cries – No words!
Or with his hound comes hallooing from the stable,
Makes love[15] with nods, and knees beneath a table;
Whose laughs are hearty, though his jests[16] are coarse,
And loves you best of all things – but his horse.
   In some fair evening, on your elbow laid,
You dream of triumphs in the rural shade;
In pensive thought recall the fancied[17] scene,
See coronations rise on every green;
Before you pass the imaginary sights
Of lords, and earls, and dukes, and gartered knights,
While the spread fan o'ershades your closing eyes;
Then give one flirt,[18] and all the vision flies.
Thus vanish sceptres, coronets, and balls,
And leave you in lone woods, or empty walls!

[1] foolish   [2] young man   [3] near   [4] part   [5] simple sewing
[6] intricately flowing   [7] between   [8] tea   [9] gaze thoughtfully
[10] attic   [11] torture   [12] cards   [13] sherry   [14] kiss   [15] flirts
[16] jokes   [17] imagined   [18] movement of the fan

What features of London life are attractive to the girl?
What kind of man must she endure in the country?
Which of Pope's vivid rhymes work best here?
Look at the description of the girl watching the clock.
Which words suggest her boredom?
Where are the antitheses in the couplets effective?

W Write a letter from Zephalinda to Pope describing her days in the country. Include ideas from the poem.

from: **The rape of the lock**

Pope could also write harshly about women. Here he presents an older woman, 'grave Clarissa', who outlines his ideas on what women should and should not be. The poem (1714) mocks the foolish lives and attitudes of the upper classes.

'Say, why are beauties praised and honoured most,
The wise man's passion, and the vain man's toast?
Why decked[1] with all that land and sea afford?[2]
Why angels called, and angel-like adored?
...
How vain are all these glories, all our pains,
Unless good sense preserve what beauty gains;
That men may say, when we the front-box[3] grace,
"Behold the first in virtue as in face!"
Oh! if to dance all night, and dress all day,
Charmed the small-pox, or chased old age away;
Who would not scorn what housewife's cares
                                    produce,
Or who would learn one earthly thing of use?
To patch,[4] nay, ogle, might become a saint,
Nor could it sure be such a sin to paint.[5]
But since, alas! frail beauty must decay,
Curled or uncurled, since locks will turn to grey;
Since painted, or not painted, all shall fade,
And she who scorns a man must die a maid;[6]
What then remains, but well our power to use.
And keep good humour still, whate'er we lose?
And trust me, dear, good humour can prevail,[7]
When airs, and flights,[8] and screams, and
                                    scolding fail.
Beauties in vain their pretty eyes may roll;
Charms strike the sight, but merit wins the soul.'

[1] dressed   [2] provide   [3] (women sat in front at the theatre
and men at the sides)   [4] to place small black patches on
the face to emphasise its good points   [5] put on make-up
[6] unmarried   [7] win   [8] tantrums

Which **PHRASES** describe the the London beauty's life?
Set against the life of the beauty are 'the housewife's
cares'. What might they be?
What dangers lie ahead of the young beauty?

from: *The ladies' defence*

The ladies' defence (1701) by Lady Mary
Chudleigh (1656-1710) was an answer to a marriage
sermon she heard, which suggested that women
should be completely ruled by men.

'Tis hard we should be by the men despised,
Yet kept from knowing what would make us
                                    prized;[1]
Debarred[2] from knowledge, banished from the
                                    schools,
And with the utmost industry[3] bred fools;
Laughed out of reason, jested[4] out of sense,
And nothing left but native innocence;
Then told we are incapable of wit,
And only for the meanest[5] drudgeries fit
...
They think, if we our thoughts can but express,
And know but how to work,[6] to dance and dress,
It is enough, as much as we should mind,[7]
As if we were for nothing else designed,
But[8] made, like puppets, to divert mankind.

The distressed poet *(1735) by William Hogarth. In*
The Dunciad, *Pope despised such feeble hacks as this
one, who cannot earn enough to pay his landlady. A
cartoon about Pope is pinned to the wall.*

O that my sex would all such toys[9] despise,
And only study to be good and wise;
...
Their memories with solid notions fill,
And let their reason dictate to their will;
Instead of novels, histories peruse,[10]
And for their guides the wiser ancients[11] choose;
Through all the labyrinths of learning go,
And grow more humble, as they more do know.
By doing this they will respect procure,[12]
Silence the men, and lasting fame secure.[13]

[1] valued   [2] kept away   [3] very carefully   [4] teased
[5] lowest   [6] sew   [7] think about   [8] only   [9] trivial things
[10] study   [11] Latin and Greek writers   [12] gain   [13] obtain

What are the women in the poem trained to be?
How do the men in the poem treat women?
What do women like Lady Mary want?
What is the poet's action plan for young women?
How does this poem answer Pope's criticisms?

D Discuss the ideas about men and women raised by
Pope and Lady Mary.

12 Thomas Gray (1716-1771): In a country churchyard

Gray had few friends and was a perfectionist in his work. He spent most of his life alone in Cambridge, where he rose to be Professor of Modern History, although he was always preparing lectures that he never gave and doing research that he never finished. Shy of human contact, he carried on his friendships through his excellent letters.

Gray was the only survivor of 12 children and was educated at Eton College, where he became close friends with Horace Walpole, later a pioneer 'Gothic' novelist. After Cambridge, he went on the Grand Tour of Europe, designed to give young men experience and culture. He quarrelled with Walpole, who preferred parties to Gray's enthusiasm for ruins, relics and views.

Gray's perfectionism limited his poetry: his complete writings, he noted with typical humour, might be 'mistaken for the works of a flea'. *ELEGY written in a country churchyard* (published in 1751) took eight years to perfect. The churchyard was loosely based on that at Stoke Poges, where his mother lived. Fittingly, Gray himself was buried there.

Elegy written in a country churchyard

In 1750 Gray sent the *Elegy* to Walpole. It became Gray's best-known poem and was much imitated. Although it is based on an elaborate web of ideas and images from other poets, CLASSICAL and modern, the poem has always been admired for its grand simplicity and truth. Samuel Johnson, the critic, said: 'The churchyard abounds with images which find a mirror in every mind, and with sentiments to which every bosom returns an echo' (*Lives of the poets: Gray*, 1781).

The curfew tolls the knell[1] of parting day,
The lowing[2] herd wind slowly o'er the lea,[3]
The ploughman homeward plods his weary way,
And leaves the world to darkness and to me.

Now fades the glimmering landscape on the sight,
And all the air a solemn stillness holds,
Save where the beetle wheels his droning flight,
And drowsy tinklings lull[4] the distant folds;[5]

Save[6] that from yonder[7] ivy-mantled[8] tower
The moping owl does to the moon complain
Of such as, wandering near her secret bower,
Molest[9] her ancient solitary reign.

[1] evening bell rings the end   [2] mooing   [3] meadow or field   [4] soothe   [5] sheep pens   [6] except   [7] over there   [8] covered   [9] disturb

What is the churchyard landscape like?
Which sights and sounds create the solemn atmosphere?

Beneath those rugged[1] elms, that yew-tree's shade,
Where heaves[2] the turf in many a mouldering heap,
Each in his narrow cell for ever laid,
The rude[3] forefathers of the hamlet[4] sleep.

The breezy call of incense-breathing morn,
The swallow twittering from the straw-built shed,
The cock's shrill clarion[5] or the echoing horn,
No more shall rouse[6] them from their lowly[7] bed.

For them no more the blazing hearth shall burn,
Or busy housewife ply[8] her evening care:
No children run to lisp their sire's[9] return,
Or climb his knees the envied kiss to share.

Oft[10] did the harvest to their sickle yield,[11]
Their furrow[12] oft the stubborn glebe[13] has broke;
How jocund[14] did they drive their team afield!
How bowed the woods beneath their sturdy[15] stroke!

[1] rough   [2] rises   [3] rough   [4] village   [5] call   [6] wake   [7] simple   [8] carry on   [9] father's   [10] often   [11] surrender   [12] mark left by a plough   [13] land   [14] joyfully   [15] strong

Who were the 'rude forefathers' of the village?
What attractive features of their lives do we hear about?
How does Gray use the word 'no'?

Let not Ambition mock their useful toil,
Their homely joys and destiny obscure;
Nor Grandeur hear, with a disdainful[1] smile,
The short and simple annals[2] of the poor.

The boast of heraldry, the pomp[3] of power,
And all that beauty, all that wealth e'er gave,
Awaits alike the inevitable hour.[4]
The paths of glory lead but to the grave.

Nor you, ye Proud, impute to these the fault,[5]
If Memory o'er their tomb no trophies raise,
Where through the long-drawn[6] aisle and fretted vault[7]
The pealing anthem swells the note of praise.

Can storied[8] urn or animated bust[9]
Back to its mansion[10] call the fleeting breath?
Can Honour's voice provoke the silent dust,
Or Flattery soothe the dull cold ear of Death?

[1] scornful   [2] stories   [3] magnificence   [4] death   [5] blame them   [6] long   [7] decorated, curved roof   [8] inscribed   [9] lively sculpture of head and shoulders   [10] body

'Ambition', 'Grandeur' and 'ye Proud' are **PERSONIFICATIONS**. They introduce wealthy, successful, upper-class people who contrast with the 'rude forefathers'. Which words tell you that Gray does not like them?
Why are the elaborate memorials of the rich inside the church pointless?

> Perhaps in this neglected spot is laid
> Some heart once pregnant with celestial fire;[1]
> Hands that the rod of empire might have swayed,[2]
> Or waked to ecstasy the living lyre.[3]
>
> But Knowledge to their eyes her ample[4] page
> Rich with the spoils of time did ne'er unroll;
> Chill Penury[5] repressed[6] their noble rage,
> And froze the genial[7] current of the soul.
>
> Full many a gem of purest ray serene
> The dark unfathomed[8] caves of ocean bear:
> Full many a flower is born to blush unseen,
> And waste its sweetness on the desert air.
>
> Some village-Hampden[9] that with dauntless
> breast[10]
>
> The little tyrant of his fields withstood;
> Some mute inglorious Milton here may rest,
> Some Cromwell guiltless of his country's blood.

[1] full of heavenly fire   [2] might have ruled an empire
[3] written poetry   [4] full   [5] poverty   [6] kept under control
[7] cheerful   [8] unmeasured   [9] champion of liberty against King Charles I   [10] fearless heart

Thomas Gray by John Eccardt (1748).

If the villagers had had more 'knowledge' ('education'), what might some of them have become?
Which two comparisons describe their frustrated lives?

> The applause of listening senates[1] to command,
> The threats of pain and ruin to despise,
> To scatter plenty[2] o'er a smiling land,
> And read their history in a nation's eyes,
>
> Their lot[3] forbade: nor circumscribed alone[4]
> Their growing virtues, but their crimes confined;
> Forbade to wade through slaughter to a throne,
> And shut the gates of mercy on mankind,
>
> The struggling pangs of conscious truth[5] to hide,
> To quench the blushes of ingenuous[6] shame,
> Or heap the shrine of Luxury and Pride
> With incense kindled at the Muse's flame.
>
> Far from the madding[7] crowd's ignoble strife[8]
> Their sober wishes never learned to stray;
> Along the cool sequestered vale[9] of life
> They kept the noiseless tenor[10] of their way.

[1] governments   [2] wealth   [3] fate   [4] did it limit only
[5] conscience   [6] honourable   [7] wild, restless   [8] humble struggles   [9] remote valley   [10] course

What good things might the villagers have done if they had become famous and important?
What wicked things might they have done?
How does the poet contrast life in the city ('madding crowd') with life in the country in the last verse?

> Yet even these bones from insult to protect
> Some frail memorial still erected nigh,[1]
> With uncouth[2] rhymes and shapeless sculpture
> decked,[3]
>
> Implores the passing tribute of a sigh.
>
> Their name, their years, spelt by the unlettered
> muse,[4]
>
> The place of fame and elegy supply:
> And many a holy text around she strews,
> That teach the rustic moralist to die.
>
> For who to dumb Forgetfulness a prey,
> This pleasing anxious being e'er resigned,
> Left the warm precincts of the cheerful day,
> Nor cast one longing lingering look behind?
>
> On some fond breast the parting soul relies,
> Some pious drops the closing eye requires;
> Even from the tomb the voice of Nature cries,
> Even in our ashes live their wonted[5] fires.

[1] nearby   [2] simple   [3] decorated   [4] half-literate poet
[5] usual

What are the memorials on the poor people's graves like?
Which line in the third verse describes life?
In the last two verses, Gray explains why the memorials are there. What reasons does he give?

A Victorian illustration to Gray's Elegy: *'Oft have we seen him at the peep of dawn'.*

For thee who, mindful of¹ the unhonoured dead,
Dost in these lines their artless² tale relate;
If chance, by lonely Contemplation³ led,
Some kindred spirit⁴ shall inquire thy fate,

Haply⁵ some hoary-headed swain⁶ may say,
'Oft have we seen him at the peep of dawn
Brushing with hasty steps the dews away
To meet the sun upon the upland lawn.

'There at the foot of yonder nodding beech
That wreathes its old fantastic roots so high,
His listless⁷ length at noontide would he stretch,
And pore upon⁸ the brook that babbles by.

'Hard by yon⁹ wood, now smiling as in scorn,
Muttering his wayward fancies¹⁰ he would rove,¹¹
Now drooping, woeful wan,¹² like one forlorn,¹³
Or crazed with care, or crossed in hopeless love.

'One morn I missed him on the customed¹⁴ hill,
Along the heath and near his favourite tree;
Another came; nor yet beside the rill,¹⁵
Nor up the lawn, nor at the wood was he;

'The next with dirges due¹⁶ in sad array¹⁷
Slow through the church-way path we saw him
                                                  borne.¹⁸
Approach and read (for thou canst read) the lay,¹⁹
Graved²⁰ on the stone beneath yon aged thorn.'

¹ remembering   ² simple   ³ thoughtful consideration
⁴ like-minded person   ⁵ perhaps   ⁶ grey-haired countryman
⁷ tired   ⁸ study closely   ⁹ near that   ¹⁰ unpredictable
ideas   ¹¹ wander   ¹² sad and pale   ¹³ miserable   ¹⁴ usual
¹⁵ brook or stream   ¹⁶ suitable mourning songs
¹⁷ funeral display   ¹⁸ carried   ¹⁹ poem   ²⁰ engraved

'Thee' seems to be Gray himself. Having
considered rich and poor, he wonders how he will
be remembered.

Where and when did the villager ('hoary-headed
swain') see the poet, and what was he doing?
The extra verse ends the poem in the manuscript:

There scatter'd oft, the earliest of the year,
By hands unseen, are show'rs of violets found;
The red-breast loves to build and warble there,
And little footsteps lightly print the ground.

Would you have included this verse? Give reasons for
your answer.

The **EPITAPH** is added on to the poem.

The epitaph

Here rests his head upon the lap of earth
A youth to Fortune and to Fame unknown.
Fair Science frowned not on his humble birth,
And Melancholy¹ marked him for her own.

Large was his bounty² and his soul sincere,
Heaven did a recompense³ as largely send:
He gave to Misery all he had, a tear,
He gained from Heaven ('twas all he wished) a
                                                  friend.

No farther seek his merits to disclose,⁴
Or draw his frailties⁵ from their dread abode,⁶
(There they alike in trembling hope repose)⁷
The bosom of his Father and his God.

¹ ('sensitivity' more than 'sadness')   ² generosity
³ reward   ⁴ make known   ⁵ weaknesses   ⁶ awe-inspiring
home   ⁷ rest

In this section the poet answers the villager. His life
was not useless. He was lonely, but used his gifts to
put into words the pity we all feel for the waste and
suffering of human life. Which line tells you this?

W Write a commentary on the line of thought in
Gray's *Elegy*.

W Write about your thoughts as you explore graves
in a churchyard. Include plenty of details about the place.

W Compare Gray's *Elegy* with other elegies in this
book: *Dark house* by Alfred Tennyson (page 58) and
Elegy by D. H. Lawrence (page 80).

D Which are your favourite verses from the poem?
Try to explain your choice.

•PART 4•

Romantic poetry

13 William Blake (1757-1827): The world of experience

In Blake's lifetime many people thought he was mad, although some devoted admirers saw his genius. He was born in London and lived there most of his life. As a child, he claimed to have seen God 'put his head to the window' and 'a tree filled with angels, bright angelic wings bespangling every bough like stars'. He was apprenticed to an engraver at 14 and learned the skill that always allowed him to earn a living. He married Catherine, a simple, illiterate woman, who would sit with him, silent for hours, as he worked at his 'very fierce inspirations' in poetry and art. Blake wrote, illustrated and engraved his own books, even hand-colouring the pages.

His first collection of poems, *Songs of Innocence*, appeared in 1789, and its twin, *Songs of Experience*, in 1794: *Songs of Innocence* offers us life as we might live it, freely and joyfully; *Songs of Experience* shows us the real world where 'iron laws', devised by Blake's grim God, crush 'the soul of sweet delight'. Sometimes Blake goes far beyond mere social commentary and attempts to show us God. In *The tyger*, Blake moves from the terror of the creature to hint at the greater terror of its creator.

Blake wrote and drew to the end of his life. His admirers kissed his door handle when they visited his shabby London rooms. He died 'singing of the things he saw in Heaven', and was buried in an unmarked grave.

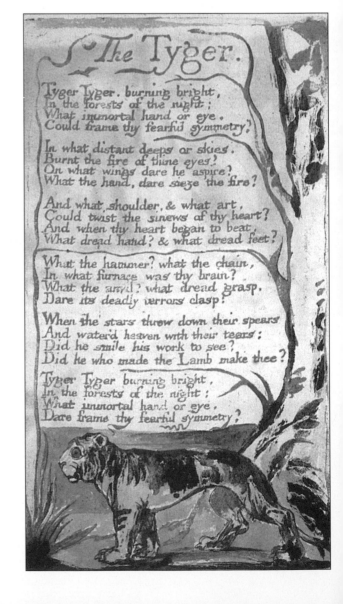

The tyger *from* Songs of Experience *(1794).*
Blake etched the poem in mirror-writing onto
a copper plate and hand-painted the prints.

London

I wander through each chartered[1] street,
Near where the chartered Thames does flow,
And mark in every face I meet
Marks of weakness, marks of woe.[2]

In every cry of every man,
In every infant's cry of fear,
In every voice, in every ban,
The mind-forged manacles[3] I hear.

How the chimney-sweeper's cry
Every blackening church appalls;
And the hapless[4] soldier's sigh
Runs in blood down palace walls.

But most through midnight streets I hear
How the youthful harlot's[5] curse
Blasts the newborn infant's tear,
And blights[6] with plagues the marriage hearse.

[1] owned by business   [2] sadness   [3] chains on hands
[4] unlucky   [5] prostitute's   [6] destroys

Sweeps often used children to climb inside chimneys to clear soot. Their street cry of 'sweep' was heard by Blake as 'weep'.

What does Blake see in people's faces in every street?
How would you explain 'mind-forged manacles'?
In what two senses is the church 'blackening'?
What should the church be doing about child labour?
Why is the soldier's blood described as being on the walls of a palace?
Even love is bought and sold. What is the effect of this on women, children and marriage?
Why is 'marriage hearse' so surprising an idea?

W What aspects of 18th-century life does Blake attack in this poem?

The Garden of Love

I went to the Garden of Love,
And saw what I never had seen:
A Chapel was built in the midst,
Where I used to play on the green.

And the gates of this Chapel were shut,
And 'Thou shalt not' writ[1] over the door;
So I turn'd to the Garden of Love
That so many sweet flowers bore;[2]

And I saw it was filled with graves,
And tomb-stones where flowers should be;
And Priests in black gowns were walking their
                                              rounds,
And binding[3] with briars my joys and desires.

[1] written   [2] produced   [3] tying up

Flowers are **SYMBOLS** of love, and the garden represents our loving relationship with God.

What other famous garden does the poem recall?
What was delightful about the Garden of Love as it used to be? How has the garden changed?
What might the Chapel be?
Why are the graves mentioned?
What effect do the details 'black' and 'walking their rounds' have on your mental picture of the priests?
Why is the word 'and' repeated in the last verse?

W Look at Samuel Palmer's painting *In a Shoreham garden* (below), which represents an earthly paradise. Write your own poem or description of it.

The sick rose

O Rose, thou art sick!
The invisible worm
That flies in the night,
In the howling storm,

Has found out thy bed
Of crimson joy:
And his dark secret love
Does thy life destroy.

In a Shoreham garden (1829) by Samuel Palmer, who shared Blake's visionary view of the natural world. The two men met in 1824.

This mysterious and passionate poem seems to be about unhappiness in human love, of which the rose is a familiar symbol. It has its twin in *Songs of Innocence*: *The blossom* is about happy, fulfilled love. In Blake's illustration, two despairing human figures hang on to the rose's branches, which are covered with thorns (the pains of love). There is also a 'catterpiller' (Blake's spelling) in the picture, which he uses elsewhere to represent the clergy.

What do you think the worm with his 'dark secret love' stands for? Is it evil destroying innocence? Marriage creating guilt in love? Satan as the snake in the Garden of Eden? People who have lost childhood happiness?

D What do you think *The sick rose* is about? Jot down your interpretation and then discuss it in a group.

W In the poems above, what does Blake tell us either about the injustices of late 18th-century England, or about human nature? Illustrate closely from at least two poems.

A poison tree

> I was angry with my friend:
> I told my wrath,[1] my wrath did end.
> I was angry with my foe:[2]
> I told it not, my wrath did grow.

And I water'd it in fears,
Night and morning with my tears;
And I sunned it with smiles,
And with soft deceitful wiles.[3]

And it grew both day and night,
Till it bore an apple bright;
And my foe beheld[4] it shine,
And he knew that it was mine,

And into my garden stole
When the night had veil'd the pole:[5]
In the morning glad I see
My foe outstretch'd beneath the tree.

[1] anger [2] enemy [3] tricks [4] saw [5] north star

What does Blake say about anger in the first verse? The word 'grow' begins the comparison that is the basis of the rest of the poem. What is this comparison? How does the **NARRATOR** 'water' and 'sun' the tree?

The apple recalls another important tree in the Bible. What is it? How does it tie in with the poem? Why is 'and' used so often? What, according to Blake, is the final result of anger? Why is 'glad' such a terrible word in this context?

D Write your own poem about anger and its results.

14 Robert Burns (1759-1796): The heaven-taught ploughman

Burns was the son of a poor farmer from Alloway in south-west Scotland. From childhood, he struggled to help his elderly father, becoming a 'dextrous ploughman for my years'. He greedily seized such education as his father and a local schoolmaster provided, and read surprisingly widely. At 15 he wrote his earliest poem to the first of the many girls that he loved: 'I never had the least thought of turning poet till I got once heartily in love, and then rhymes and song were the spontaneous language of my heart'.

His first book, *Poems Chiefly in the Scottish Dialect* (1786), brought him success, after many years of failure in farming. He was invited to Edinburgh and praised as 'the heaven-taught ploughman'. His poems shared the lives and thoughts of ordinary working people, written in

'his and their native language'. The young Walter Scott (1771-1832), another great Scottish writer, saw him in Edinburgh in his best farmer's buckskin breeches and long boots, and noticed how his eyes 'glowed when he spoke with feeling or interest'.

In his last years, Burns collected and reworked traditional Scottish songs. He died of rheumatic fever, probably caused by the hardships of his early life.

*from: **Man was made to mourn: A dirge**[1]*

In this poem Burns anticipates the sympathy he was to feel for the French Revolution. 'Man's inhumanity to Man' became a catch phrase of the times. He borrowed his title from an old song that his mother sang to her blind uncle, who sobbed as he heard the chorus, 'Man was made to moan'.

When chill November's surly[2] blast
   Made fields and forests bare,
One ev'ning, as I wander'd forth,
   Along the banks of Aire,[3]
I spy'd a man, whose aged step
   Seem'd weary, worn with care;
His face was furrow'd o'er[4] with years,
   And hoary[5] was his hair.

[1] sad song [2] unfriendly [3] a Scottish river [4] wrinkled
[5] grey

'Young stranger, whither[1] wand'rest thou?'
   Began the rev'rend Sage;[2]
'Does thirst of wealth thy step constrain,[3]
   Or youthful pleasure's rage?
Or haply,[4] prest with cares and woes,
   Too soon thou hast began,
To wander forth, with me, to mourn
   The miseries of Man.

[1] where [2] respected wise man [3] control [4] perhaps

The sun that overhangs yon[1] moors,
   Out-spreading far and wide,
Where hundreds labour to support
   A haughty lordling's[2] pride;
I've seen yon[3] weary winter-sun
   Twice forty times return;
And ev'ry time has added proofs,
   That Man was made to mourn.

[1] those [2] arrogant young lord's [3] that

...
Many and sharp the num'rous ills
   Inwoven with our frame![1]
More pointed still we make ourselves,
   Regret, remorse and shame!
And Man, whose heav'n-erected[2] face,
   The smiles of love adorn,
Man's inhumanity[3] to Man
   Makes countless thousands mourn!

[1] body [2] made by God [3] cruelty

See yonder poor, o'erlabour'd wight,[1]
   So abject,[2] mean[3] and vile,[4]
Who begs a brother of the earth
   To give him leave to toil;[5]
And see his lordly fellow-worm,
   The poor petition spurn,[6]
Unmindful,[7] tho' a weeping wife,
   And helpless offspring[8] mourn.

[1] overworked man [2] without self-respect [3] poor
[4] shameful [5] work [6] request reject [7] uncaring
[8] children

If I'm design'd yon lordling's slave,
   By Nature's law design'd,
Why was an independent wish
   E'er planted in my mind?
If not, why am I subject to
   His cruelty, or scorn?
Or why has Man the will and pow'r
   To make his fellow mourn?

Yet let not this too much, my son,
   Disturb thy youthful breast:
This partial view of human-kind
   Is surely not the last!
The poor, oppressed, honest man
   Had never, sure, been born,
Had there not been some recompense[1]
   To comfort those that mourn!

O Death! the poor man's dearest friend,
   The kindest and the best!
Welcome the hour, my aged limbs
   Are laid with thee at rest!
The great, the wealthy fear thy blow,
   From pomp[2] and pleasure torn;
But Oh! a blest relief for those
   That weary-laden[3] mourn!'

[1] reward [2] magnificent display [3] tired and weighed
down

How does the setting reflect the **THEME**?
What sort of person is the speaker?
What are the 'ills/Inwoven with our frame'?
Where do you see 'Man's inhumanity to Man' today?
What grim reward is there for the poor?

D   What might the young man say in reply about the
pleasures and satisfactions of life?

*Robert Burns in Alexander Reid's portrait, painted
a year before his death.*

To a mouse, on turning her up in her nest with the plough November 1785

Wee, sleeket,[1] cowran,[2] tim'rous[3] beastie,
O, what a panic's in thy breastie!
Thou need na start awa[4] sae hasty,
    Wi' bickering brattle![5]
I wad be laith[6] to rin an' chase thee,
    Wi' murdering pattle![7]

[1] sleek [2] cowering [3] shy and fearful [4] away [5] rushing
haste [6] reluctant [7] spade (used to clean a plough)

I'm truly sorry Man's dominion[1]
Has broken Nature's social union,
An' justifies that ill opinion,
    Which makes thee startle,
At me, thy poor, earth-born companion,
    An' fellow-mortal!

I doubt na, whyles,[2] but thou may thieve;
What then? poor beastie, thou maun live!
A daimen-icker[3] in a thrave[4]
    'S a sma' request:
I'll get a blessin wi' the lave,[5]
    An' never miss't!

[1] rule [2] sometimes [3] ear of corn [4] two stooks of corn
[5] rest

Thy wee-bit[1] housie, too, in ruin!
It's silly wa's[2] the win's[3] are strewin!
An' naething, now, to big a new ane,[4]
    O' foggage[5] green!
An' bleak December's winds ensuin,[6]
    Baith snell an' keen![7]

[1] little [2] walls [3] winds [4] build a new one
[5] rough grass [6] following [7] bitter and cutting

Thou saw the fields laid bare an' wast,
An' weary Winter comin fast,
An' cozie here, beneath the blast,
    Thou thought to dwell,
Till crash! the cruel coulter[1] past
    Out thro' thy cell.

[1] plough blade

That wee-bit heap o' leaves an' stibble,
Has cost thee monie a weary nibble!
Now thou's turn'd out, for a' thy trouble,
    But house or hald,[1]
To thole[2] the Winter's sleety dribble,
    An' cranreuch[3] cauld!

[1] holding [2] endure [3] frost

But Mousie, thou art no thy-lane,[1]
In proving foresight may be vain:
The best laid schemes o' Mice an' Men,
    Gang aft agley,[2]
An' lea'e us nought but grief an' pain,
    For promis'd joy!

[1] alone [2] often go off course

Still, thou art blest, compar'd wi' me!
The present only toucheth thee:
But Och! I backward cast my e'e,[1]
    On prospects drear![2]
An' forward, tho' I canna see,
    I guess an' fear!

[1] eyes [2] miserable

Why does Burns forgive the mouse the damage to the farm?
Why is the destruction of the nest so sad?
What lessons about life does Burns see in the incident?
Why is the poor farmer worse off than the mouse?

D Role play an interview with Burns about the mouse.

W Write a detailed commentary on Burns's thought and method in this poem.

My luve is like a red, red rose

My luve is like a red, red rose,
 That's newly sprung in June:
My luve is like the melodie,
 That's sweetly play'd in tune.
As fair art thou, my bonie[1] lass,
 So deep in luve am I,
And I will luve thee still, my dear,
 Till a' the seas gang[2] dry.

Till a' the seas gang dry, my dear,
 And the rocks melt wi' the sun!
And I will luve thee still, my dear,
 While the sands o' life shall run.
And fare-thee-weel, my only luve,
 And fare-the-weel a while!
And I will come again, my luve,
 Tho' it were ten-thousand mile.

[1] beautiful [2] go

This is one of the songs that Burns collected and improved. 'The rocks melt wi' the sun' is a dramatic vision of the end of the earth as it crashes into the sun.

How are repetition and **HYPERBOLE** used in the song?

W Write a story based on the parting of man and woman indicated in this song.

15 William Wordsworth (1770-1850): Nature and humanity

Wordsworth was born at Cockermouth and went to school in the heart of the Lake District. Although he was orphaned at 13, he enjoyed a wonderful childhood, free to explore the hills and lakes, experiences he describes in his long poem *The prelude*.

After studying at Cambridge University, he went to France where he saw and sympathised with the French Revolution. A legacy allowed him to settle in Somerset with his beloved sister, Dorothy (1771-1855). There they worked with Samuel Coleridge to produce *Lyrical BALLADS* (1798). These poems were revolutionary because they described 'incidents of common life' and ordinary people, and were written in deliberately plain words, 'the real language of men'.

Wordsworth saw London as 'a monstrous ant hill', a 'too busy world'. In *The reverie of poor Susan,* Susan is one of the thousands of country people who came to the city for work. The poem was also inspired by the caged thrushes kept outside London shops. Its rhythm imitates that of street ballads.

Dorothy Wordsworth: a silhouette, the only complete portrait of her as a young woman.

The reverie[1] of poor Susan

At the corner of Wood-Street[2], when day-light appears,
There's a thrush that sings loud, it has sung for three years:
Poor Susan has pass'd by the spot and has heard m
In the silence of morning the song of the bird.

'Tis a note of enchantment; what ails[3] her? She sees
A mountain ascending, a vision of trees;
Bright volumes of vapour through Lothbury[2] glide,
And a river flows on through the vale[4] of Cheapside.[2]

Green pastures she views in the midst of the dale,[4]
Down which she so often has tripp'd[5] with her pail,
And a single small cottage, a nest like a dove's;
The only one dwelling on earth that she loves.

She looks, and her heart is in heaven, but they fade,
The mist and the river, the hill and the shade;
The stream will not flow, and the hill will not rise,
And the colours have all pass'd away from her eyes.

Poor outcast![6] return – to receive thee once more
The house of thy father will open its door,
And thou once again, in thy plain russet[7] gown,
May'st hear the thrush sing from a tree of its own.

[1] daydream [2] (streets in London) [3] troubles [4] valley
[5] skipped [6] person forced to leave home
[7] reddish-brown rough cloth

What can you tell about Susan and her life story from the poem?
What memories does the thrush bring back to her?
What happens to Susan's vision?
How are the young woman and the thrush linked?

W Tell the full story of Susan and her unhappy exile. Use the incidents in the poem to start and end your **NARRATIVE**.

In 1799 William and Dorothy moved back to the Lake District, settling in Dove Cottage, Grasmere. William wrote some of his finest poems there, often inspired by Dorothy's journal, in which she described everything they did, felt and saw.

Dorothy was content to help and inspire her brother, who paid tribute to her: 'She gave me eyes, she gave me ears'. Coleridge thought her 'exquisite ... her eye watchful in minutest observation of nature'. She wrote the first notes for William's daffodil poem. After visiting friends on Ullswater, they walked home along the lake where they saw thousands of wild daffodils in bloom.

Thursday April 15 1802

When we were in the woods ... we saw a few daffodils close to the water side. We fancied that the lake had floated the seeds ashore and that the little colony[1] had so sprung up. But as we went along there were more and yet more and at last under the boughs of the trees, we saw that there was a long belt of them along the shore, about the breadth of a country turnpike road.[2] I never saw daffodils so beautiful they grew among the mossy stones about and about them, some rested their heads upon these stones as on a pillow for weariness and the rest tossed and reeled[3] and danced and seemed as if they verily[4] laughed with the wind that blew upon them over the lake, they looked so gay[5] ever glancing[6] ever changing.

[1] group   [2] high road   [3] whirled around   [4] really   [5] happy
[6] catching light

Two years later, William wrote his poem.

I wandered lonely as a cloud
That floats on high o'er vales[1] and hills,
When all at once I saw a crowd,
A host,[2] of golden daffodils;
Beside the lake, beneath the trees,
Fluttering and dancing in the breeze.

Continuous as the stars that shine
And twinkle on the Milky Way,
They stretched in never-ending line
Along the margin[3] of a bay:
Ten thousand saw I at a glance,
Tossing their heads in sprightly[4] dance.

The waves beside them danced, but they
Out-did the sparkling waves in glee:[5]
A poet could not but be gay,[6]
In such a jocund[7] company:
I gazed – and gazed – but little thought
What wealth the show to me had brought:

For oft, when on my couch I lie
In vacant[8] or in pensive[9] mood,
They flash upon that inward eye
Which is the bliss of solitude;
And then my heart with pleasure fills,
And dances with the daffodils.

[1] valleys   [2] great number   [3] edge   [4] lively   [5] delight
[6] merry   [7] joyful   [8] relaxed   [9] thoughtful

What comparisons does Wordsworth borrow from Dorothy to describe the flowers? What other similarities are there between the poem and the passage? What are the differences?
What is the poet's 'inward eye'? How does he like to use it on the daffodils? What exactly does Wordsworth like to remember about the flowers?

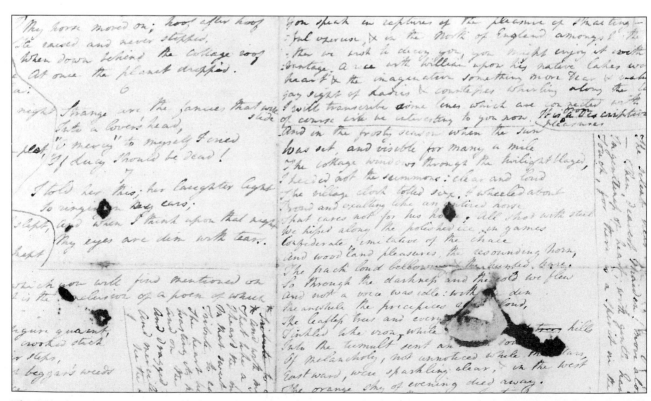

The Groslar Letter (1798), in which Wordsworth sent several of his latest poems, including parts of the Lucy Poems *(left) and* The prelude *(right), to Coleridge in Germany.*

In 1798 the Wordsworths and Coleridge went to Groslar in Germany, where William began to write the *Lucy Poems*, a sequence of 'little **RHYME** poems' that outlines a relationship between the **NARRATOR** and a girl who suddenly dies. Was Lucy real? Coleridge guessed cleverly: 'Most probably in some gloomier moment he had fancied the moment in which his sister might die'.

She dwelt among the untrodden ways

She dwelt[1] among the untrodden ways
  Beside the springs of[2] Dove,
A Maid whom there were none to praise
  And very few to love:

A violet by a mossy stone
  Half hidden from the eye!
– Fair as a star, when only one
  Is shining in the sky.

She lived unknown, and few could know
  When Lucy ceased to be;[3]
But she is in her grave, and, oh,
  The difference to me!

[1] lived   [2] source of the river   [3] stopped existing

What is Lucy's home background?
What two comparisons describe Lucy? Why are they appropriate? Which word is avoided in the last verse? Why is the last line understated?

A slumber did my spirit seal

A slumber did my spirit seal;[1]
  I had no human fears:
She seemed a thing that could not feel
  The touch of earthly years.

No motion has she now, no force;[2]
  She neither hears nor sees;
Rolled round in earth's diurnal[3] course,
  With rocks, and stones, and trees.

[1] sleep kept worries shut away   [2] strength   [3] daily

Why are the 's' sounds effective in the first line?
What has Lucy become in the second verse?
Why are the words 'no' and 'and' repeated?
Which word is avoided again?
What picture of Lucy is given in the first verse? What in the second? What happens between the verses?

W Write a detailed analysis of the *Lucy Poems* above, describing their subject matter and anything that interests you in Wordsworth's language and **STYLE**.

W Write a story about the relationship of the narrator and Lucy. Use background detail from the poems, but add ideas from your imagination – about how they met, or how exactly she died, for example.

D Role play an interview with Wordsworth about Lucy.

16 Samuel Coleridge (1772-1834): The damaged archangel

To Wordsworth, Coleridge was 'the most wonderful man I have ever known'. Charles Lamb (1775-1834), the essayist, thought he was like 'an archangel – a little damaged'. Although Coleridge tended not to finish his ambitious literary projects, partly through 'constitutional indolence' and partly because he was addicted to opium, he was still a very influential **ROMANTIC** writer.

His father, a Devonshire clergyman, died when Coleridge was nine. Coleridge became a 'playless daydreamer' at Christ's Hospital school in London. At Cambridge University, his debts forced him to join the army, under the strange name of Silas Tomkyn Comberbache.

He married and settled at Nether Stowey in Somerset. There he worked closely with William and Dorothy Wordsworth to produce *Lyrical* **BALLADS** (1798), to which he contributed his supernatural verse tale, *The rime of the ancient mariner*.

By 1802 Coleridge had written his best poetry and turned to criticism: 'The poet is dead in me ... I was once a volume of gold leaf rising and riding in every breath of **FANCY**'. He was saved from the worst effects of his opium addiction by a London doctor, at whose house he lived until his death.

Frost at midnight

In 1798 Coleridge was living in Nether Stowey. His marriage had become unhappy, but he loved his children dearly. Hartley (named after a famous philosopher) was the eldest. He is the baby in *Frost at midnight*, in which his education is considered.

The frost performs its secret ministry,[1]
Unhelped by any wind. The owlet's cry
Came loud – and hark,[2] again! loud as before.
The inmates of[3] my cottage, all at rest,
Have left me to that solitude, which suits
Abstruser musings:[4] save that at my side
My cradled infant slumbers peacefully.
'Tis calm indeed! so calm, that it disturbs
And vexes meditation[5] with its strange
And extreme silentness. Sea, hill, and wood,

This populous village! Sea, and hill, and wood,
With all the numberless goings-on of life,
Inaudible as dreams! the thin blue flame
Lies on my low-burnt fire, and quivers not;
Only that film,⁶ which fluttered on the grate,
Still flutters there, the sole unquiet thing.
Methinks, its motion in this hush of nature
Gives it dim sympathies with me who live,
Making it a companionable form,
Whose puny flaps and freaks the idling Spirit
By its own moods interprets, every where
Echo or mirror seeking of itself,
And makes a toy of thought.

¹teaching   ²listen   ³people who live in   ⁴more
complicated thinking   ⁵disturbs deep thought   ⁶smoke

What can Coleridge see and hear around him, inside
and outside the cottage?
The poet's mind is still active. To what other moving
things does he relate it?

                              But O! how oft,¹
How oft, at school, with most believing mind,
Presageful,² have I gazed upon the bars,
To watch that fluttering stranger!³ and as oft
With unclosed lids,⁴ already had I dreamt
Of my sweet birth-place, and the old church-tower,
Whose bells, the poor man's only music, rang
From morn to evening, all the hot Fair-day,
So sweetly, that they stirred and haunted me

*Samuel Coleridge, the brilliant young lecturer and
poet, in 1795: portrait by Peter Van Dyke.*

With a wild pleasure, falling on mine ear
Most like articulate⁵ sounds of things to come!
So gazed I, till the soothing things, I dreamt,
Lulled me to sleep, and sleep prolonged my dreams!
And so I brooded all the following morn,
Awed⁶ by the stern preceptor's⁷ face, mine eye
Fixed with mock study on my swimming⁸ book:
Save if the door half opened, and I snatched
A hasty glance, and still my heart leaped up,
For still I hoped to see the stranger's face,
Townsman, or aunt, or sister more beloved,
My play-mate when we both were clothed alike!⁹

¹often   ²full of a sense of what is about to happen
³(by superstition, thin smoke on a low fire showed that
a stranger was about to arrive)   ⁴open eyes   ⁵clearly
spoken   ⁶made afraid   ⁷instructor's   ⁸out of focus
⁹when we were very young (young boys and girls wore
similar clothes)

What does Coleridge love about his home town?
What impression is given of school? Which words
create this? Who does the poet miss most from home?

   Dear Babe, that sleepest cradled by my side,
Whose gentle breathings, heard in this deep calm,
Fill up the interspersed vacancies¹
And momentary² pauses of the thought!
My babe so beautiful! it thrills my heart
With tender gladness, thus to look at thee,
And think that thou shalt learn far other lore,³
And in far other scenes! For I was reared
In the great city, pent 'mid⁴ cloisters dim,
And saw nought lovely but the sky and stars.
But thou, my babe! shalt wander like a breeze
By lakes and sandy shores, beneath the crags
Of ancient mountain, and beneath the clouds,
Which image in their bulk⁵ both lakes and shores
And mountain crags: so shalt thou see and hear
The lovely shapes and sounds intelligible⁶
Of that eternal language, which thy God
Utters, who from eternity doth teach
Himself in all, and all things in himself.
Great universal teacher! he shall mould
Thy spirit, and by giving make it ask.

   Therefore all seasons shall be sweet to thee,
Whether the summer clothe the general earth
With greenness, or the redbreast sit and sing
Betwixt the tufts of snow on the bare branch
Of mossy apple-tree, while the nigh⁷ thatch
Smokes⁸ in the sun-thaw; whether the cave-
                                        drops fall
Heard only in the trances of the blast,⁹
Or if the secret ministry of frost
Shall hang them up in silent icicles,
Quietly shining to the quiet moon.

¹scattered gaps in a line of thought   ²short
³knowledge   ⁴imprisoned in   ⁵in their size are like
⁶that can be understood   ⁷nearby   ⁸steams
⁹pauses in the wind

Which sound takes the poet's mind back to his baby? Coleridge wants a better education for the baby, given by nature itself. How does he intend to rear his child? What great lessons will nature teach the boy? Which lines tell us that Coleridge believed that God exists in nature?

W Trace the line of thought through the poem, explaining Coleridge's ideas about good and bad education.

W Write your own poem about nature, showing some of the things that the seasons 'make sweet' to you. Try to use realistic detail as Coleridge does.

In 1797 Coleridge went to stay in a lonely house near Porlock to recover from ill health. At that time the dangerous drug, opium, was often taken as a medicine, and it was opium that produced Coleridge's extraordinary *Kubla Khan*, a 'vision in a dream; a fragment'. He described how he wrote it and why it was not finished:

The fantastic visions produced by the drug opium: a 19th-century print.

In consequence[1] of a slight indisposition,[2] an anodyne[3] had been prescribed, from the effects of which [the author] fell asleep in his chair at the moment that he was reading the following sentence, or words of the same substance, in *Purchas's Pilgrimage*:[4] 'Here the Khan Kubla commanded a palace to be built, and a stately[5] garden thereunto.[6] And thus ten miles of fertile ground were inclosed[7] with a wall'. The Author continued for about three hours in a profound[8] sleep, at least of the external senses, during which time he has the most vivid confidence,[9] that he could not have composed less than from two to three hundred lines; if that indeed can be called composition in which all the images rose up before him as things, with a parallel production of the correspondent expressions,[10] without any sensation or consciousness of effort. On awaking he appeared to himself to have a distinct recollection[11] of the whole, and taking his pen, ink, and paper, instantly and eagerly wrote down the lines that are here preserved. At this moment he was unfortunately called out by a person on business from Porlock, and detained by him above an hour, and on his return to his room, found, to his no small surprise and mortification, that though he still retained some vague and dim recollection of the general purport[12] of the vision, yet, with the exception of some eight or ten scattered lines and images, all the rest had passed away like the images on the surface of a stream into which a stone has been cast, but, alas! without the after restoration of the latter![13]

[1] as a result [2] illness [3] drug that relieves pain
[4] (a travel book of 1613) [5] grand [6] next to it
[7] surrounded [8] deep [9] belief [10] at the same time as the words came to him [11] clear memory [12] meaning
[13] without returning to its previous state, like the stream

Kubla Khan

In Xanadu did Kubla Khan
A stately pleasure-dome decree:[1]
Where Alph, the sacred river, ran
Through caverns measureless[2] to man
  Down to a sunless sea.
So twice five miles of fertile ground
With walls and towers were girdled round:[3]
And there were gardens bright with sinuous rills,[4]
Where blossomed many an incense-bearing tree;
And here were forests ancient as the hills,
Enfolding sunny spots of greenery.

But oh! that deep romantic chasm[5] which slanted
Down the green hill athwart a cedarn cover![6]
A savage place! as holy and enchanted
As e'er beneath a waning[7] moon was haunted
By woman wailing for her demon-lover!
And from this chasm, with ceaseless turmoil
           seething,[8]

As if this earth in fast thick pants were breathing,
A mighty fountain momently[9] was forced:
Amid whose swift half-intermitted[10] burst
Huge fragments vaulted[11] like rebounding[12] hail,
Or chaffy grain beneath the thresher's[13] flail:
And 'mid these dancing rocks at once and ever
It flung up momently the sacred river.
Five miles meandering with a mazy motion[14]
Through wood and dale the sacred river ran,
Then reached the caverns measureless to man,
And sank in tumult[15] to a lifeless ocean:
And 'mid this tumult Kubla heard from far
Ancestral voices prophesying war![16]
   The shadow of the dome of pleasure
   Floated midway on the waves;
   Where was heard the mingled measure
   From the fountain and the caves.
It was a miracle of rare device,[17]
A sunny pleasure-dome with caves of ice!

   A damsel[18] with a dulcimer[19]
   In a vision once I saw:
   It was an Abyssinian maid,
   And on her dulcimer she played,
   Singing of Mount Abora.
   Could I revive within me
   Her symphony and song,
   To such a deep delight 'twould win me,
That with music loud and long,
I would build that dome in air,
That sunny dome! those caves of ice!
And all who heard should see them there,
And all should cry, Beware! Beware!
His flashing eyes, his floating hair!
Weave a circle round him thrice,

And close your eyes with holy dread,
For he on honey-dew hath fed,
And drunk the milk of Paradise.

[1] order   [2] limitless   [3] surrounded   [4] curving streams
[5] very deep, narrow opening in the ground   [6] across an
area planted with cedar trees   [7] becoming gradually
smaller   [8] foaming and bubbling   [9] from moment to
moment   [10] stopping and starting   [11] jumped
[12] bouncing back   [13] person who hits grain with a tool
(= flail) to remove its outer layer (= chaff)   [14] curving in
a complicated pattern   [15] loud noise   [16] the voices of his
dead relatives foretelling war   [17] made with unusual skill
[18] girl   [19] a musical instrument

The poem makes a tremendous impression, especially, with its changing rhythms, **ALLITERATION** and strange names, when it is read aloud. Yet no one is able to say what it is about. It is very dream-like with its detail, colour and sudden changes, from the pleasure-dome to thc damsel, and then to the striking poet-prophet.

D Discuss what you find impressive and mysterious in *Kubla Khan*. What meaning do you find in the poem? Which lines do you like the best?

W Look at some of the descriptive **PHRASES** in the poem, for example: 'stately pleasure-dome'; 'sunless sea'; 'gardens bright with sinuous rills'; 'sunny spots of greenery'; 'deep romantic chasm'; 'mighty fountain'; 'sunny pleasure-dome with caves of ice'. What pictures do the phrases create in your mind? Next, imagine you are walking through the landscape around the pleasure-dome. Describe what you see, hear and feel, around you. Use Coleridge's words and ideas, but also add some of your own.

17 George Gordon, Lord Byron (1788-1824): The end of the world

When Byron's poem *Childe Harold's pilgrimage*, a description of his youthful travels in Albania, Greece and Turkey, was published in 1812, Byron 'awoke one day to find [him]self famous'. His title, inherited at the age of 10, had brought him only a half-empty 'melancholy mansion', but the huge sales of his poetry made him wealthy.

Byron had a lame leg, but was a social star and enormously attractive to women. However, an unwise marriage and scandal about his personal life drove him abroad. He left England in 1816, never to return. His restless wanderings in Switzerland and Italy are described in his letters, which are now valued, perhaps, more than his poetry.

He continued to compose, adding to *Childe Harold* (1816-17), writing *Manfred* (1817), and inventing a new hero based on himself in *Don Juan* (1819-1824). Although he still used the **VERSE FORM** imitated from Spenser's *Faerie Queene*, he added his own humorous **COLLOQUIAL STYLE**.

What is the end of Fame? 'tis but to fill
  A certain portion of uncertain paper:
Some liken it to climbing up a hill,
  Whose summit, like all hills, is lost in vapour;
For this men write, speak, preach, and heroes kill,
    And bards burn what they call their 'midnight
                taper',
To have, when the original is dust,
A name, a wretched picture and worse bust.

What are the hopes of man? Old Egypt's King
  Cheops erected the first Pyramid
And largest, thinking it was just the thing
  To keep his memory whole, and mummy hid;
But somebody or other rummaging,
  Burglariously broke his coffin's lid:
Let not a monument give you or me hopes,
Since not a pinch of dust remains of Cheops.

(from: Don Juan, canto 1)

Byron became involved in the Greek struggle to be independent of the Turkish empire, of which Greece was then part. He was invited to become leader of the Greeks at Missolonghi, but he died of rheumatic fever before the fighting began. Despite his immense European popularity, he was refused burial in Westminster Abbey. Only in 1969 was he allowed a memorial there.

Darkness

In 1816 Byron was living in Switzerland. The younger poet, Shelley, and his wife, Mary, were staying nearby. A wet summer kept them indoors and Byron suggested they should all write ghost stories. Mary wrote the best, *Frankenstein* (published 1818), which is based on a fearful dream. When the Shelleys left for Italy, Byron wrote *Darkness*, a poem about the end of life on earth. He also claimed to have been inspired by a dream, but some critics have detected details from a German novel he might have read.

I had a dream, which was not all a dream.
The bright sun was extinguish'd, and the stars
Did wander darkling[1] in the eternal space,
Rayless, and pathless, and the icy earth
Swung blind and blackening in the moonless air;
Morn came and went – and came, and brought
                no day,
And men forgot their passions in the dread
Of this their desolation;[2] and all hearts
Were chill'd into a selfish prayer for light:
And they did live by watchfires – and the thrones,
The palaces of crowned kings – the huts,
The habitations of all things which dwell,
Were burnt for beacons; cities were consumed,
And men were gather'd round their blazing homes
To look once more into each other's face;
Happy were those who dwelt within the eye
Of the volcanos, and their mountain-torch:

Lord Byron in Albanian national costume, after his visit to the Near East in 1809-1811: portrait by Thomas Phillips.

A fearful hope was all the world contain'd;
Forests were set on fire – but hour by hour
They fell and faded – and the crackling trunks
Extinguish'd with a crash – and all was black.
The brows[3] of men by the despairing light
Wore an unearthly aspect,[4] as by fits[5]
The flashes fell upon them; some lay down
And hid their eyes and wept; and some did rest
Their chins upon their clenched[6] hands, and
                smiled;
And others hurried to and fro, and fed
Their funeral piles with fuel, and look'd up
With mad disquietude[7] on the dull sky,
The pall[8] of a past world; and then again
With curses cast them down upon the dust,
And gnash'd their teeth and howl'd: the wild
              birds shriek'd,
And, terrified, did flutter on the ground,
And flap their useless wings; the wildest brutes
Came tame and tremulous;[9] and vipers crawl'd
And twined themselves among the multitude,[10]
Hissing, but stingless – they were slain[11] for food!
And War, which for a moment was no more,
Did glut[12] himself again: – a meal was bought
With blood, and each sate sullenly apart
Gorging himself in gloom: no love was left;
All earth was but one thought – and that was death
Immediate and inglorious;[13] and the pang
Of famine fed upon all entrails – men
Died, and their bones were tombless as their flesh:
The meagre[14] by the meagre were devour'd,
Even dogs assail'd[15] their masters, all save one,

And he was faithful to a corse, and kept
The birds and beasts and famish'd men at bay,
Till hunger clung[16] them, or the dropping dead
Lured[17] their lank[18] jaws; himself sought out no
food,
But with a piteous and perpetual moan,
And a quick desolate cry, licking the hand
Which answer'd not with a caress – he died.
The crowd was famish'd by degrees; but two
Of an enormous city did survive,
And they were enemies: they met beside
The dying embers[19] of an altar-place
Where had been heap'd a mass of holy things
For an unholy usage; they raked up,
And shivering scraped with their cold skeleton
hands
The feeble ashes, and their feeble breath
Blew for a little life, and made a flame
Which was a mockery; then they lifted up
Their eyes as it grew lighter, and beheld[20]
Each other's aspects[21] – saw, and shriek'd, and
died –
Even of their mutual hideousness they died,[22]
Unknowing who he was upon whose brow
Famine had written Fiend. The world was void,[23]
The populous and the powerful was a lump,
Seasonless, herbless, treeless, manless, lifeless,
A lump of death – a chaos[24] of hard clay.
The rivers, lakes, and ocean all stood still,
And nothing stirr'd within their silent depths;
Ships sailorless lay rotting on the sea,
And their masts fell down piecemeal: as they
dropp'd
They slept on the abyss without a surge –
The waves were dead; the tides were in their grave,
The moon, their mistress, had expired before;
The winds were wither'd in the stagnant[25] air,
And the clouds perish'd; Darkness had no need
Of aid from them – She was the Universe.

[1] growing darker   [2] sadness and loneliness   [3] faces
[4] ghostly expression   [5] now and then   [6] squeezed shut
[7] worry   [8] cloth covering a coffin   [9] shaking   [10] crowd
[11] killed   [12] stuff   [13] shameful   [14] thin   [15] attacked
[16] shrivelled   [17] attracted   [18] thin   [19] glowing pieces
[20] saw   [21] faces   [22] they died because they both looked
so ugly   [23] empty   [24] complete confusion   [25] still

What disaster has happened?
What desperate things do the people do to make light?
Which people think themselves lucky?
How do people behave?
What happens to wild creatures?
What one example of courage and dignity is described?

What vivid details does Byron give in his final pictures of the dying earth?
Collect some words used in the poem that relate to violence, panic, desperation and fear.
Which section of the poem do you find most impressive, and why?

W Write the story of the two survivors in the huge city.

W Write the diary of someone living through Byron's darkness disaster. Use details from the poem.

D Create a radio programme dealing with the Darkness disaster. Interview survivors who describe what happened.

W Use details from the poem and the drawing by the French artist Doré (below) to compose your own piece on the theme of the last person alive.

A 'last man' image (1872) by Gustave Doré: The New Zealander sketches the ruins of London.

18 Percy Bysshe Shelley (1792-1822): Reflection and revolution

Shelley's short life was full of scandal and rebellion. He had two reputations: he was either 'a base, bad man', 'the vilest wretch now living', who drove his young wife to suicide; or he was the idealist, considered by Byron to be 'the best and least selfish man I ever knew'.

Shelley was born into a wealthy Sussex family and was sent down from Oxford University for writing a pamphlet supporting atheism. He offended his family further by eloping with Harriet Westbrook, a 16-year-old friend of his sisters. As they wandered the country, Shelley began to write poetry and spoke out for political reform; he even sent out pamphlets by hot-air balloon. He befriended an important thinker on reform, William Godwin (1756-1836), and fell in love with his daughter, Mary. In 1816 Harriet drowned herself and the scandal forced Shelley to spend the rest of his life in Italy, where he wrote his best-known poems, including *Prometheus unbound* (1820) and *Adonais* (1821), his ELEGY for John Keats.

Shelley enjoyed sailing his boat *Ariel*. One day he was caught in a storm and drowned. When his body was washed ashore, he was known only by his clothes and the books in his pocket. His friends burned his body on a beach:

More wine was poured over Shelley's body than he had consumed during his life. As the back of the head rested on the red-hot bottom bars of the furnace, the brains literally seethed, bubbled and boiled. What surprised us all was that the heart remained entire.

(Edward Trelawny:
Records of Shelley, Byron and the Author, 1878)

ODE *to the west wind*

Shelley noted that the poem 'was conceived and chiefly written in a wood ... near Florence, and on a day when that tempestuous wind ... was collecting the vapours which pour down autumnal rains'. In the poem, the wind is a **METAPHOR** for coming revolution. As it blows from the west, Shelley is thinking of the successful American Revolution.

1

O Wild West Wind, thou breath of Autumn's being,[1]
  Thou from whose unseen presence the leaves
                                 dead
Are driven like ghosts from an enchanter[2] fleeing,

  Yellow, and black, and pale, and hectic[3] red,
Pestilence-stricken multitudes![4] O thou
  Who chariotest[5] to their dark wintry bed

The wingèd seeds, where they lie cold and low,
  Each like a corpse within its grave, until
Thine azure[6] sister of the Spring shall blow

  Her clarion[7] o'er the dreaming earth, and fill
(Driving sweet buds like flocks to feed in air)
  With living hues[8] and odours plain and hill;

Wild Spirit, which art moving everywhere;
Destroyer and preserver; hear, O hear!

[1] existence   [2] wizard   [3] feverish   [4] sick crowds   [5] drives
[6] blue   [7] trumpet   [8] colours

The first section describes the effect of the wind on leaves. To what are the leaves and wind compared?
Why is the wind 'destroyer and preserver'?
How is the 'sister' of the West Wind described?

Lord Byron watches as Shelley's body is burned on an Italian beach: painting (1889) by Louis Fournier.

2

Thou on whose stream,[1] 'mid the steep sky's
commotion,
  Loose clouds like earth's decaying leaves are shed,
Shook from the tangled boughs of heaven and
ocean,

  Angels of rain and lightning! there are spread
On the blue surface of thine airy surge,[2]
  Like the bright hair uplifted from the head

Of some fierce Maenad,[3] even from the dim verge[4]
  Of the horizon to the zenith's height,[5]
The locks[6] of the approaching storm. Thou dirge[7]

  Of the dying year, to which this closing night
Will be the dome of a vast sepulchre,[8]
  Vaulted[9] with all thy congregated might[10]

Of vapours,[11] from whose solid atmosphere
Black rain, and fire, and hail will burst: O hear!

[1] air current [2] wave [3] wild, excited follower of Bacchus,
god of wine [4] edge [5] high part of sky [6] hair [7] song
for the dead [8] huge tomb [9] strengthened
[10] collected power [11] clouds

The second section describes the wind's effects on the
air. How are the clouds blown by the wind described?
What will the wind bring with it later?

3

Thou who didst waken from his summer dreams
  The blue Mediterranean, where he lay,
Lulled[1] by the coil[2] of his crystalline streams,

  Besides a pumice[3] isle in Baiae's[4] bay,
And saw in sleep old palaces and towers
  Quivering within the wave's intenser day,[5]

All overgrown with azure moss, and flowers
  So sweet, the sense faints picturing them! Thou
For whose path the Atlantic's level powers

  Cleave[6] themselves into chasms,[7] while far
below
The sea-blooms and the oozy woods which wear
  The sapless foliage of the ocean, know

Thy voice, and suddenly grow gray with fear,
And tremble and despoil themselves:[8] O hear!

[1] calmed [2] twisting currents [3] made from lava
[4] (a Roman sea resort near Naples, the ruins of which are
now underwater) [5] darker blue [6] split
[7] deep, narrow openings [8] lose their shape

The third section describes the effect of the wind on
water. It even affects the underwater world of the
Mediterranean: how does the vegetation there change?
Look at the next two sections. What aspects of
revolution could each be describing?

4

If I were a dead leaf thou mightest bear;
  If I were a swift cloud to fly with thee;
A wave to pant beneath thy power, and share

  The impulse[1] of thy strength, only less free
Than thou, O uncontrollable! if even
  I were as in my boyhood, and could be

The comrade of thy wanderings over heaven,
  As then, when to outstrip thy skiey[2] speed
Scarce seemed a vision – I would ne'er have striven

  As thus with thee in prayer in my sore[3] need.
O! lift me as a wave, a leaf, a cloud!
  I fall upon the thorns of life! I bleed!

A heavy weight of hours has chained and bowed
One too like thee – tameless,[4] and swift, and proud.

5

Make me thy lyre,[5] even as the forest is:
  What if my leaves arc falling like its own?
The tumult[6] of thy mighty harmonies[7]

  Will take from both a deep autumnal tone,
Sweet though in sadness. Be thou, Spirit fierce,
  My spirit! Be thou me, impetuous[8] one!

Drive my dead thoughts over the universe,
  Like withered leaves, to quicken[9] a new birth;
And, by the incantation[10] of this verse,

  Scatter, as from an unextinguished hearth[11]
Ashes and sparks, my words among mankind!
  Be through my lips to unawakened earth

The trumpet of a prophecy! O Wind,
If Winter comes, can Spring be far behind?

[1] force [2] in the air [3] extreme [4] wild [5] (an Aeolian lyre
is a stringed instrument that makes a sound when the
wind blows over its strings) [6] loud, confused noise
[7] powerful music [8] hasty [9] give life to [10] spell
[11] still burning fire

In what ways was the poet like the wind? How has he
changed?
What does Shelley want the wind to do in the fifth
section?
What does the poet want to do with the thoughts and
words of his poetry?
What is the coming spring predicted in the last line?
The poem is written as a set of five sonnets. Trace the
complex **RHYME** scheme in each.

W Describe how Shelley deals with the ideas of social
injustice and possible revolution.

Ozymandias[1]

Shelley saw the exhibition of relics from ancient
Egypt, including a huge granite figure of Pharaoh
Rameses II, at the British Museum in 1817. He
went to the exhibition with a poet friend and they
both wrote **SONNETS** on the **THEME** of relics
decaying in the desert.

The mystery of the relics of ancient Egypt is described in Ozymandias: The Sphinx *(1854) by William Holman Hunt.*

I met a traveller from an antique land
Who said: Two vast and trunkless[2] legs of stone
Stand in the desert ... Near them, on the sand,
Half sunk, a shattered visage[3] lies, whose frown,
And wrinkled lip, and sneer of cold command,
Tell that its sculptor well those passions read
Which yet survive, stamped on these lifeless things,
The hand[4] that mocked them, and the heart[5]
                                                            that fed:
And on the pedestal[6] these words appear:
'My name is Ozymandias, king of kings:
Look on my works, ye Mighty, and despair!'
Nothing beside remains. Round the decay
Of that colossal wreck, boundless[7] and bare
The lone and level sands stretch far away.

[1] (Greek name for Rameses II)   [2] without a body   [3] face
[4] (of sculptor)   [5] (of Ozymandias)   [6] base   [7] unlimited

What is left of the statue? What is the most impressive relic? What does it tell us about Rameses? What does the message on the pedestal mean? Why do the last three lines make the poem **IRONIC**? What comment does the poem make on the pride of kings?

D Interview the traveller. Ask him or her to describe the statue and its setting. Discuss the meaning of the ironic message on the pedestal.

19 John Keats (1795-1821): Beauty is truth

Keats, son of a London stable manager, became an orphan at 15 and found the family fortune tied up in lawsuits, but he was lucky in his education at an enlightened boarding school in Enfield. In 1814 Charles Cowden Clarke, the headmaster's son, introduced him to Spenser's *Faerie Queene*, which he read with excitement 'like a young horse turned into a spring meadow'. He wrote his first poem and told his brothers that if he could not be a poet he would kill himself. He had, however, already begun work as a trainee surgeon at Guy's Hospital, London.

In 1816 his **SONNET** *On first looking into Chapman's Homer* was praised by the poet and journalist Leigh Hunt (1784-1859), who said it 'completely announced the new poet taking

possession'. Like many others, he was attracted by Keats's face with its 'eager power', 'in which energy and sensibility were mixed up'. To the disgust of his guardian, Keats abandoned medicine, and his first poems were published in 1817.

Endymion (1818), an ambitious **CLASSICAL** poem, followed, with its famous opening: 'A thing of beauty is a joy for ever'. Some critics from important literary magazines now savaged him brutally:

It is a better and a wiser thing to be a starved apothecary than a starved poet; so back to the shop Mr John, back to plasters, pills and ointment boxes.

(*Blackwood's Edinburgh Magazine*, August 1818)

John Keats, sketched by his artist friend, Benjamin Haydon, in 1816.

Keats was hurt, but could still write confidently in one of his remarkable letters to friends: 'I think I shall be among the English poets at my death'.

When his brother Tom died of tuberculosis in 1818, Keats went to live Hampstead, where he met Fanny Browne and fell in love. 'I cannot exist without you – you have absorbed me', he told her in a letter. Although he was sick and poor, in 1819 he produced his best work: *The eve of St Agnes*, **ODE** *to a nightingale*, *Ode to a Grecian urn* and *To autumn*. He wrote as if he knew time was short. In 1820 he coughed blood: he too had tuberculosis. 'That drop of blood is my death warrant', he wrote to a friend. 'I must die.'

Encouraged by Shelley to live in a warmer climate, he arranged to go to Italy. 'The thought of leaving Miss Browne is beyond everything horrible', he told a friend. He got as far as Rome, where he died. He was buried in the Protestant Cemetery there under his own **EPITAPH**: 'Here lies one whose name was writ in water'.

To autumn

The poem opens very early in autumn, just after the harvest. Keats described his inspiration:

How beautiful the season is now – how fine the air. A temperate sharpness about it. I never liked stubble fields so much as now – Aye better than the chilly green of the spring. Somehow a

stubble plain looks warm – this struck me so much in my Sunday's walk that I composed upon it.

(letter of 21 September 1819)

Season of mists and mellow[1] fruitfulness!
  Close bosom-friend of the maturing sun;[2]
Conspiring[3] with him how to load and bless
  With fruit the vines that round the thatch-eaves
                 run;
To bend with apples the mossed cottage-trees,
  And fill all fruit with ripeness to the core;
    To swell the gourd, and plump the hazel
                 shells
With a sweet kernel;[4] to set budding more,
  And still more, later flowers for the bees,
  Until they think warm days will never cease,
    For Summer has o'erbrimmed[5] their
                 clammy[6] cells.

Who hath not seen thee oft amid[7] thy store?
  Sometimes whoever seeks abroad may find
Thee sitting careless on a granary floor,
  Thy hair soft-lifted by the winnowing[8] wind,
Or on a half-reaped furrow[9] sound asleep,
  Drowsed with the fume of poppies, while thy
                 hook[10]
    Spares the next swath[11] and all its twinèd
                 flowers;
And sometimes like a gleaner[12] thou dost keep
  Steady thy laden head across a brook;
  Or by a cider-press, with patient look,
    Thou watchest the last oozings hours by hours.

Where are the songs of Spring? Ay, where are they?
  Think not of them, thou hast thy music too, –
While barred clouds bloom the soft-dying day,
  And touch the stubble-plains[13] with rosy hue;[14]
Then in a wailful choir the small gnats mourn
  Among the river sallows,[15] borne aloft
    Or sinking as the light wind lives or dies;
And full-grown lambs loud bleat from hilly bourn;[16]
  Hedge-crickets sing; and now with treble soft
  The redbreast whistles from a garden-croft;
    And gathering swallows twitter in the skies.

[1] ripe   [2] sun that creates ripeness   [3] plotting   [4] nut
[5] filled so full that they overflow   [6] wet and sticky (i.e. full of honey)   [7] in   [8] sorting grain from chaff   [9] mark made in the ground by a plough   [10] sickle (a knife with a curved blade and short handle)   [11] width cut by a sickle
[12] person who gathers what is left of a crop after harvesting   [13] fields covered with cut crops after the harvest   [14] colour   [15] willows   [16] stream

Keats greets autumn, who is **PERSONIFIED** as a close friend of the sun.

The **THEME** here is fruitfulness. List the examples of autumn's fruitfulness in cottage gardens.
The harvest seems almost too good. Which words suggest this?

Keats's poem To autumn *was inspired by harvest fields near Winchester in September 1819.* The reapers *(1865) by John Linnell echoes the themes and moods of the poem.*

ONOMATOPOEIA is boldly used here: the words with 'o' or 'u' sounds suggest fatness and ripeness. Find some. In the second verse, autumn appears as a human figure, probably female, carrying on the last work of the harvest. How is autumn's tiredness suggested by the many 's' and 'z' sounds here? Find them.
Why is 'soft-lifted' so vivid?
The three verses show the movement of time from early to late autumn. What is the theme of the last verse? Where is the coming of winter, even death, hinted at in the last verse?

D Keats talks of the 'songs of Spring'. What do you find the most delightful and interesting features of each of the seasons?

W Write a detailed review of this poem, commenting on its ideas and delicate technique.

W Compose your own poem or short prose sketch on autumn in the town or country.

Ode to a nightingale

In spring 1819 Keats was living with his friend Charles Brown in Hampstead. Brown remembered how

a nightingale had built her nest near my house. Keats felt a continual and tranquil joy in her song; and one morning he took a chair from the breakfast-table to the grass plot under a plum tree ... when he came into the house, I perceived he had some scraps of paper in his hand ...

On these was the first draft of the *Nightingale* poem.

1

My heart aches, and a drowsy[1] numbness pains
    My sense, as though of hemlock[2] I had drunk,
Or emptied some dull opiate[3] to the drains
    One minute past, and Lethe-wards[4] had sunk:
'Tis not through envy of thy happy lot,[5]
    But being too happy in thine happiness, –
        That thou, light-winged Dryad[6] of the trees,
            In some melodious[7] plot
Of beechen green, and shadows numberless,
    Singest of summer in full-throated ease.[8]

[1] sleepy [2] poison [3] drug that makes you sleepy
[4] towards the river of death and oblivion [5] fortune
[6] wood nymph [7] full of music [8] relaxed and with your whole voice

What are Keats's feelings?
How does the nightingale affect him?

2

O, for a draught[1] of vintage![2] that hath been
    Cool'd a long age in the deep-delved[3] earth,
Tasting of Flora[4] and the country green,
    Dance, and Provençal[5] song, and sunburnt mirth![6]
O for a beaker full of the warm South,

Full of the true, the blushful Hippocrene,[7]
  With beaded bubbles winking at the brim,
    And purple-stained mouth;
That I might drink, and leave the world unseen,
And with thee fade away into the forest dim:

3

Fade far away, dissolve, and quite forget
  What thou among the leaves hast never known,
The weariness, the fever, and the fret
  Here, where men sit and hear each other groan;
Where palsy[8] shakes a few, sad, last gray hairs,
  Where youth grows pale, and spectre-thin,[9]
                    and dies;
    Where but to think is to be full of sorrow
      And leaden-eyed despairs,
    Where Beauty cannot keep her lustrous[10] eyes,
    Or new Love pine at [11] them beyond to-morrow.

[1] drink   [2] wine   [3] dug deep   [4] the goddess of flowers
[5] (from the Provence area in France)   [6] laughter
[7] fountain sacred to goddesses of poetry in Greek myth
[8] an illness of old age   [9] as thin as a ghost (this may refer
to Keats's brother Tom, who had just died)   [10] full of light
[11] long for

Keats is very good at making things seem real to the
physical senses. Find examples of this in verse 2.
How does Keats's mood change in verse 2?
What sad thoughts on human life are there in verse 3?

4

Away! away! for I will fly to thee,
  Not charioted[1] by Bacchus[2] and his pards,[3]
But on the viewless[4] wings of Poesy,[5]
  Though the dull[6] brain perplexes and retards:
Already with thee! tender is the night,
  And haply[7] the Queen-Moon is on her throne,
    Cluster'd around by all her starry Fays;[8]
      But here there is no light,
Save[9] what from heaven is with the breezes blown
    Through verdurous[10] glooms and winding
                   mossy ways.

5

I cannot see what flowers are at my feet,
  Nor what soft incense hangs upon the boughs,
But, in embalmed[11] darkness, guess each sweet
  Wherewith[12] the seasonable[13] month endows[14]
The grass, the thicket, and the fruit-tree wild;
  White hawthorn, and the pastoral eglantine;[15]
    Fast fading violets cover'd up in leaves;
    And mid-May's eldest child,
  The coming musk-rose,[16] full of dewy wine,
  The murmurous haunt of flies on summer eves.

[1] transported   [2] the god of wine   [3] leopards   [4] invisible
[5] poetry   [6] stupid   [7] perhaps   [8] attendants   [9] except for
[10] green   [11] heavy with scent   [12] that   [13] suited to the
season   [14] gives to   [15] honeysuckle   [16] white rose that
smells very sweet

Keats sets aside wine and devotes himself to
creating a joy like the bird's by writing his own
poetry.

What lovely things does he see, and smell, around him?
How is onomatopoeia used in this description?

6

Darkling[1] I listen; and, for many a time
  I have been half in love with easeful[2] Death,
Call'd him soft names in many a mused[3] rhyme,
  To take into the air my quiet breath;
Now more than ever seems it rich to die,
  To cease upon the midnight with no pain,
    While thou art pouring forth thy soul abroad
      In such an ecstasy!
  Still wouldst thou sing, and I have ears in vain –
    To thy high requiem[4] become a sod.[5]

7

Thou wast not born for death, immortal Bird!
  No hungry generations tread thee down;
The voice I hear this passing night was heard
  In ancient days by emperor and clown:
Perhaps the self-same song that found a path
  Through the sad heart of Ruth,[6] when, sick for
                     home,
    She stood in tears amid the alien corn;
      The same that oft-times hath
  Charm'd magic casements,[7] opening on the
                    foam
  Of perilous[8] seas, in faery lands forlorn.[9]

[1] in the darkness   [2] easy and relaxing   [3] thought
[4] service for dead   [5] piece of turf   [6] (in the Bible story,
Ruth travelled to Bethlehem to help with the harvest
after her husband died)   [7] windows   [8] dangerous
[9] deserted

Verse 6 expresses Keats's wish to die. Which words
make it seem pleasant to die?
When would the poet most like to die? Why?
The last two lines are about magical fairy stories
involving nightingales. What pictures in your mind do
'magic casements' and 'foam of perilous seas' create?
What effect does the last word have on the mood of
the poem?

8

Forlorn! the very word is like a bell
  To toll[1] me back from thee to my sole self!
Adieu![2] the fancy[3] cannot cheat so well
  As she is fam'd to do, deceiving elf.
Adieu! adieu! thy plaintive anthem[4] fades
  Past the near meadows, over the still stream,
    Up the hill-side; and now 'tis buried deep
    In the next valley-glades:[5]
  Was it a vision, or a waking dream?
    Fled is that music: – Do I wake or sleep?

[1] ring or call   [2] goodbye   [3] idea   [4] touching song
[5] open places in forests

The bird moves away and the song fades. The last sentence asks a key question: which is more real and important, the beauty of the nightingale's singing, the vision it gives of things beyond life, and the delight it creates in the listener, or the reality of the everyday world?

W Which parts of this poem do you find most powerful and moving? Say why.

W In your own words, try to follow Keats's thoughts as he listens to the nightingale.

20 John Clare (1793-1864): Asylum poems

Clare was the 'Northamptonshire peasant poet' who became famous for a short time in 1820 because of his *Poems Descriptive of Rural Life and Scenery*. He was the son of a poor labourer. As a boy, he loved the countryside around his native Helpston:

> I often lingered a minute on the woodland stile to hear the wood pigeons clapping their wings among the dark oaks I hunted curious flowers in rapture ... I felt the beauty of these with eager delight but I knew nothing of poetry It was felt and not uttered.

(from: *Autobiography*, 1826)

John Clare, the mentally ill poet, painted at Northampton Aslyum in 1844 by Thomas Grimshawe, a local artist.

Clare was inspired to write poems by James Thomson's *The Seasons*. A lucky contact with a London publisher encouraged his 'restless hope of being something better than a ploughman'. His first collection sold well. He went to London as a celebrity and met some of the leading writers of the time. Fashions change, and a reviewer of his second book questioned the value of poems by 'ploughmen, milkmaids and other such prodigies'. Clare was sent back to his cottage. Although disappointed, he continued to write, reaching a peak with the vivid *Shepherd's Calendar* (1827), a picture of country life through the seasons.

In 1832 his family was rehoused. Clare was already upset about the effects of enclosure and changes in farming on the local countryside and felt like a stranger in his new environment. By 1837 his depression had become mental illness. He was removed to an asylum and entered a 'land of shadows', where he thought he was Byron, Burns, Lord Nelson, or a famous boxer. In 1841 he escaped and walked home, writing a haunting description of his journey. He hoped to find his boyhood sweetheart, Mary Joyce, but she had died unmarried years before.

In 1841 his wife Patty could no longer cope. Clare was officially stated to be mentally ill and sent to Northampton General Lunatic Asylum, where he remained in 'imprisonment', unvisited by his family. The doctors who decided that Clare was mentally ill noted his years 'addicted to poetical prosing'. Those in the asylum were more sympathetic and encouraged his poetry. The superintendent remembered how 'on one occasion he presented me with the following scrap: "Where flowers are, God is, and I am free!"'

Between 1841 and 1860, Clare wrote around 850 poems. After 1860 the poems died away. Clare told a visitor: 'They have cut off my head and picked out all the letters of the alphabet – and brought them out through my ears, and then they want me to write poetry!'

I am

1

I am – yet what I am, none cares or knows;
   My friends forsake[1] me like a memory lost: –
I am the self-consumer of my woes;[2] –
   They rise and vanish in oblivion's host,
Like shadows in love's frenzied stifled throes:[3] –
And yet I am, and live – like vapours tost

2

Into the nothingness of scorn and noise, –
   Into the living sea of waking dreams,
Where there is neither sense of life or joys,
   But the vast shipwreck of my lifes esteems;[4]
Even the dearest, that I love the best
Are strange – nay, rather stranger than the rest.

3

I long for scenes, where man hath never trod
   A placc where woman never smiled or wept
There to abide[5] with my Creator, God;
   And sleep as I in childhood, sweetly slept,
Untroubling, and untroubled where I lie,
The grass below – above the vaulted[6] sky.

[1] abandon   [2] suffer alone   [3] mad sufferings   [4] opinions
[5] live   [6] rounded

Clare gives an extraordinary picture of what it is like to be mentally ill. He only knows he exists, having lost all other sense of identity. The poem seems to echo his letter of 1848 to Mary: 'there is no faith here so I hold my tongue and wait the end without attention or intention – I am that I am'.

'I am' occurs three times in verse 1. What does it mean?
What does the poet not know about himself?
How is Clare the 'self-consumer' of his woes?
To what other pain in life is madness compared in verse 2?
How does the rhythm change in verse 3?
The last verse describes Clare's idea of heaven. What is it like? How would he feel there?

D   Where are the poet's friends and family? What reasons could there be for their behaviour?

Sometimes Clare used the natural world as a **METAPHOR** for his moods and feelings.

Hesperus

Hesperus,[1] the day is gone
Soft falls the silent dew
A tear is now on many a flower
And heaven lives in you

Hesperus, the evening mild
Falls round us soft and sweet
'Tis like the breathings of a child
When day and evening meet

Hesperus, the closing flower
Sleeps on the dewy ground
While dews fall in a silent shower
And heaven breathes around

Hesperus, thy twinkling ray
Beams in the blue of heaven
And tells the traveller on his way
That earth shall be forgiven

[1] the evening star

What parts of *Hesperus* are like *I am*?
What are Clare's feelings about life on earth?
Which words and sounds create the calm mood?

To John Clare is one of Clare's last poems, dated February 1860. The 'John Clare' mentioned might be his son, but is more likely to be his childhood self. He vividly recalls a morning of his childhood.

To John Clare

Well, honest John, how fare you[1] now at home?
The spring is come and birds are building nests
The old cock-robin to the stye is come
With olive feathers and its ruddy breast[2]
And the old cock with wattles[3] and red comb[4]
Struts[5] with the hens and seems to like some best
Then crows and looks about for little crumbs
Swept out by little folks an hour ago
The pigs sleep in the sty the bookman[6] comes
The little boy lets home-close-nesting[7] go
And pockets tops and tawes[8] where daiseys bloom
To look at the new number[9] just laid down
With lots of pictures and good stories too
And Jack the jiant-killer's high renown[10]

[1] are you getting on   [2] red chest   [3] loose folds of skin on the throat   [4] fleshy growth on top of a cock's head   [5] walks proudly   [6] person who travelled around selling cheap books   [7] bird-nesting in the fields near home   [8] toys   [9] latest cheap child's book   [10] fame

What season is it?
What delights of home are mentioned?
Who are the 'little folks'?
Why does the boy give up hunting birds' nests that morning?
What are the pleasures of the simple cheap book sold to the boy by the pedlar?
How does this poem resemble *I am*?

W   Which is the most impressive and moving of Clare's asylum poems? Give detailed evidence to support your choice.

•PART 5•

Victorian voices

21 Alfred Tennyson (1809-1892): A romance and *In memoriam*

Tennyson was one of 12 children and was born at Somersby, a remote village in the Lincolnshire Wolds. His father, the local rector, encouraged his children to write. 'Before I could read', recalled Tennyson, 'I was in the habit on a stormy day of spreading my arms to the wind, and crying out "I hear a voice that's speaking in the wind" and the words "far, far away" had always a strange charm for me'. It was not a happy household: the rector drank heavily and Tennyson's brothers' minds were, he said, 'delicately organised': later, two became insane, and one an opium addict.

Tennyson was glad to escape to Cambridge University in 1827. There he wrote a prize poem, which, said a critic, showed 'really first rate genius', and met Arthur Hallam, another poet, who became his best friend. Tennyson's first published collections of 1830 and 1832 included *The Lady of Shalott*, the first of his many Arthurian stories. The poems were attacked by the crude critics of the time and described as 'drivel, dismal drivel'. This, and Hallam's sudden death in 1833, led to a 10-year silence when he wrote but did not publish. It was the 1842 collection that established him as a great poet. *In memoriam A. H. H.*, his extraordinary sequence of poems reflecting on the death of Hallam, appeared in 1850. It won the praise of Queen Victoria herself, 'who valued it next to the Bible', and he later became **POET LAUREATE**.

Tennyson had met his future wife Emily when she was 17. Only when she was 37 and he 40, did they marry and settle in a fine house on the Isle of Wight. He became Lord Tennyson in 1883, the only English poet to receive a title just for writing poetry.

The Lady of Shalott

Look carefully at the picture on the cover of this book and note the details. Think about the story of the woman in the boat. When might the story be set? Why might she be in the boat? Where might she have come from? Where might she be going? Is she happy or not?

Part 1

On either side the river lie
Long fields of barley and of rye,
That clothe the wold[1] and meet the sky;
And through the field the road runs by
    To many-towered Camelot;
And up and down the people go,
Gazing where the lilies blow[2]
Round an island there below,
    The island of Shalott.

Willows whiten, aspens[3] quiver,
Little breezes dusk and shiver
Through the wave that runs for ever
By the island in the river
    Flowing down to Camelot.
Four gray walls, and four gray towers,
Overlook a space of flowers,
And the silent isle imbowers[4]
    The Lady of Shalott.

By the margin,[5] willow-veiled,
Slide the heavy barges trailed[6]
By slow horses; and unhailed[7]
The shallop[8] flitteth[9] silken-sailed
    Skimming down to Camelot:
But who hath seen her wave her hand?
Or at the casement[10] seen her stand?
Or is she known in all the land,
    The Lady of Shalott?

Only reapers,[11] reaping early
In among the bearded barley,
Hear a song that echoes cheerly[12]
From the river winding clearly,
    Down to towered Camelot:
And by the moon the reaper weary,[13]
Piling sheaves[14] in uplands airy,
Listening, whispers ''Tis the fairy
    Lady of Shalott.'

[1] open, rolling country [2] flower [3] poplars [4] shelters
[5] edge [6] dragged [7] not called to by anyone [8] boat
[9] moves lightly and quickly [10] window [11] people who
harvest [12] cheerfully [13] tired [14] bundles of corn

Make some notes about the landscape near the island.
What is so mysterious about the island and the Lady?

Part 2

There she weaves by night and day
A magic web[1] with colours gay.[2]
She has heard a whisper say,
A curse is on her if she stay[3]
    To look down to Camelot.
She knows not what the curse may be,
And so she weaveth steadily,
And little other care hath she,
    The Lady of Shalott.

And moving through a mirror clear
That hangs before her all the year,
Shadows of the world appear.
There she sees the highway near
    Winding down to Camelot:
There the river eddy[4] whirls,
And there the surly[5] village-churls,[6]
And the red cloaks of market girls,
    Pass onward from Shalott.

Sometimes a troop of damsels[7] glad,
An abbot[8] on an ambling pad,[9]
Sometimes a curly shepherd-lad,
Or long-haired page in crimson clad,[10]
    Goes by to towered Camelot;
And sometimes through the mirror blue
The knights come riding two and two:
She hath no loyal knight and true,
    The Lady of Shalott.

But in her web she still delights
To weave the mirror's magic sights,
For often through the silent nights
A funeral, with plumes[11] and lights
    And music, went to Camelot:
Or when the moon was overhead,
Came two young lovers lately wed;
'I am half sick of shadows,' said
    The Lady of Shalott.

[1] fabric [2] bright [3] stops (weaving) [4] small whirlpool
[5] bad-tempered [6] farm labourers [7] young unmarried
women [8] important priest [9] horse that moves slowly
[10] clothed [11] feathers

What does the Lady do all day?
The mirror helps her see the pattern on her weaving
from the other side. What else does she use it for?
What are her feelings about the lovers and the knights?
Who do you think put the curse on the Lady? Why?

Part 3

A bow-shot[1] from her bower-eaves,[2]
He rode between the barley-sheaves,
The sun came dazzling through the leaves,
And flamed upon the brazen greaves[3]
    Of bold Sir Lancelot.
A red-cross knight for ever kneeled
To a lady in his shield,
That sparkled on the yellow field,
    Beside remote Shalott.

The gemmy bridle[4] glittered free,
Like to some branch of stars we see
Hung in the golden Galaxy.[5]
The bridle bells rang merrily
    As he rode down to Camelot:
And from his blazoned[6] baldric[7] slung
A mighty silver bugle[8] hung,
And as he rode his armour rung,
    Beside remote Shalott.

All in the blue unclouded weather
Thick-jewelled shone the saddle-leather,
The helmet and the helmet-feather
Burned like one burning flame together,
    As he rode down to Camelot.
As often through the purple night,
Below the starry clusters bright,
Some bearded meteor, trailing light,
    Moves over still Shalott.

His broad clear brow[9] in sunlight glowed;
On burnished[10] hooves his war-horse trode;
From underneath his helmet flowed
His coal-black curls as on he rode,
    As he rode down to Camelot.
From the bank and from the river
He flashed into the crystal mirror,
'Tirra lirra,' by the river
    Sang Sir Lancelot.

She left the web, she left the loom,[11]
She made three paces through the room,
She saw the water-lily bloom,
She saw the helmet and the plume,
    She looked down to Camelot.
Out flew the web and floated wide;
The mirror cracked from side to side;
'The curse is come upon me,' cried
    The Lady of Shalott.

[1] as far away as an arrow is shot from a bow [2] house
[3] brass armour protecting the lower leg [4] leather strips
on a horse's head [5] star system [6] decorated with
heraldry [7] sash worn over the shoulder to carry a sword
[8] musical instrument like a trumpet [9] forehead
[10] polished, shiny [11] frame on which thread is woven

Describe Sir Lancelot.
What comparisons are used to describe him?
Why is he so impressive?
Lancelot is reflected in the river and in the mirror.
What effect does this have on the Lady and on the mirror?
How does the Lady bring the curse on herself?

D What might the curse be? What might happen next?

'She left the web, she left the loom': The Lady of Shalott *(1894), painted by John Waterhouse.*

Part 4

In the stormy east-wind straining,
The pale yellow woods were waning,[1]
The broad stream in his banks complaining,
Heavily the low sky raining
    Over towered Camelot;
Down she came and found a boat
Beneath a willow left afloat,
And round about the prow[2] she wrote
    The Lady of Shalott.

And down the river's dim expanse
Like some bold seër[3] in a trance,[4]
Seeing all his own mischance[5] –
With a glassy countenance[6]
    Did she look to Camelot.
And at the closing of the day
She loosed[7] the chain, and down she lay;
The broad stream bore[8] her far away,
    The Lady of Shalott.

Lying, robed in snowy white
That loosely flew to left and right –
The leaves upon her falling light –
Through the noises of the night
    She floated down to Camelot:
And as the boat-head wound along
The willowy hills and fields among,
They heard her singing her last song,
    The Lady of Shalott.

Heard a carol[9], mournful, holy,
Chanted loudly, chanted lowly,
Till her blood was frozen slowly,
And her eyes were darkened wholly,[10]
    Turned to towered Camelot.
For ere she reached upon the tide
The first house by the water-side,
Singing in her song she died,
    The Lady of Shalott.

Under tower and balcony,
By garden-wall and gallery,[11]
A gleaming shape she floated by,
Dead-pale between the houses high,
    Silent into Camelot.
Out upon the wharfs[12] they came,
Knight and burgher,[13] lord and dame,[14]
And round the prow they read her name,
    The Lady of Shalott.

Who is this? and what is here?
And in the lighted palace near
Died the sound of royal cheer;[15]
And they crossed themselves[16] for fear,
    All the knights at Camelot:
But Lancelot mused a little space;[17]
He said, 'She has a lovely face;
God in his mercy lend her grace,
    The Lady of Shalott.'

[1] fading [2] front part of the boat [3] prophet [4] vision
[5] bad luck [6] face [7] undid [8] carried [9] song
[10] completely [11] covered passageway [12] platforms built along the shore [13] citizen [14] lady [15] feasting [16] made the sign of the cross [17] thought for a short time

How and why does the weather change?
Why does the Lady die?
Why are the closing lines so sad?
How does each of the four sections end?
Early critics wanted a hidden meaning behind the story. Is there one?

W You are one of the citizens of Camelot. You watch the boat arrive. Then you visit the island and the Lady's room and piece together the story. Include plenty of background detail from the poem.

D Talk with some of the people who saw parts of the Lady's story: a bargeman, a reaper, one of the passers-by on the road, Sir Lancelot. They describe what they have seen and heard of the Lady and her strange fate.

from: *In memoriam A. H. H.*

A. H. H. was Tennyson's great friend, Arthur Hallam, who died unexpectedly in 1833. Tennyson wrote the first of his 131 *In memoriam* poems a few days later, adding to the collection over many years. It was a diary of grief that turned into a discussion of the point and meaning of life. Tennyson added a religious conclusion, but horror at death seems more important. 'Its faith is a poor thing', noted the poet T. S. Eliot, 'but its doubt is a very intense experience'.

2

Old Yew, which graspest at the stones
   That name the under-lying dead,
   Thy fibres[1] net the dreamless head,
Thy roots are wrapt about the bones.

The seasons bring the flower again,
   And bring the firstling[2] to the flock;[3]
   And in the dusk of thee, the clock
Beats out the little lives of men.

O not for thee the glow, the bloom,
   Who changest not in any gale,
   Nor branding[4] summer suns avail[5]
To touch thy thousand years of gloom:

And gazing on thee, sullen[6] tree,
   Sick for thy stubborn hardihood,[7]
   I seem to fail from out my blood[8]
And grow incorporate into[9] thee.

[1] thin roots [2] lamb [3] group of sheep [4] burning [5] are of any use [6] gloomy [7] toughness [8] die away from my life [9] become part of

The mood of In memoriam: Can these dry bones live? *(1856) by Henry Bowler. As the girl looks at the skull, a young tree shoots from the grave marked 'Resurgam' ('I will live again'*

The dark evergreen yew tree traditionally grows in churchyards. What does Tennyson imagine the tree doing to the dead?

Why is the **PHRASE** 'dreamless head' frightening?

What changes in the second verse? What stays the same in the third verse?

What is the yew a **SYMBOL** of in the last verse?

7

Dark house, by which once more I stand
  Here in the long unlovely street,
  Doors, where my heart was used to beat
So quickly, waiting for a hand,

A hand that can be clasped[1] no more –
  Behold[2] me, for I cannot sleep,
  And like a guilty thing I creep
At earliest morning to the door.

He is not here; but far away
  The noise of life begins again,
  And ghastly[3] through the drizzling rain
On the bald[4] street breaks the blank[5] day.

[1] held [2] see [3] pale and unhealthy [4] bare [5] empty

In this poem Tennyson revisits Hallam's London home.

What does the fact that the house is dark mean?

Why are doors mentioned?

What is powerful about the mention of the hand?

Why has the poet come to the house?

Why does the 'noise of life' seem pointless to Tennyson?

The last verse pulls back from the dark house to show a wider scene. What effect does this have?

115

Now fades the last long streak of snow,
  Now burgeons[1] every maze of quick[2]
  About the flowering squares, and thick
By ashen[3] roots the violets blow.[4]

Now rings the woodland loud and long,
  The distance takes a lovelier hue,[5]
  And drowned in yonder living blue
The lark becomes a sightless[6] song.

Now dance the lights on lawn and lea,[7]
  The flocks are whiter down the vale,[8]
  And milkier every milky sail
On winding stream or distant sea;

Where now the seamew pipes,[9] or dives
  In yonder greening gleam,[10] and fly
  The happy birds, that change their sky
To build and brood;[11] that live their lives

From land to land; and in my breast
  Spring wakens too; and my regret
  Becomes an April violet,
And buds and blossoms like the rest.

[1] sprouts [2] hawthorn hedge [3] pale grey [4] flower
[5] colour [6] invisible [7] field [8] valley [9] seagull makes a sharp sound [10] the sea [11] hatch eggs

What is happening to the natural world?

What is happening to Tennyson's grief?

Compare this poem with *Dark house* above.

W Write about the various ideas and moods in the *In memoriam* poems, making clear what impresses you about their content and technique. Which is the best poem?

22 Emily Brontë (1818-1848): A peculiar music

After their mother and two sisters had died, the Brontë children – Charlotte, Branwell, Emily and Anne – remained at home with their clergyman father at Haworth Parsonage, Yorkshire. They formed 'a little society among themselves', and enjoyed writing stories about the fantasy countries, Glasstown and Gondal, that they invented.

These stories became more complex as they grew up. A drawing made in 1837 shows Emily and Anne working at stories of 'Emperors and Empresses of Gondal'. Emily's poetry began as the thoughts of these characters, especially those of 'Augusta Geraldine Almeda' (A. G. A.). Anne noticed

that Emily kept some poems hidden: 'She is writing some poetry too. I wonder what it is about?' Emily kept two notebooks, Gondal and personal. Charlotte found one of them by accident: 'I thought [the poems] condensed and terse, vigorous and genuine. To my ear, they also had a peculiar music – wild, melancholy and elevating' (*Biographical Note on Emily*, 1850).

When Emily recovered from her anger at this discovery, the sisters agreed to publish their poems together. They chose pen-names, keeping their initials: Currer, Ellis and Acton Bell. Only two copies were sold when the poems were published in 1846, but one reviewer noticed Emily's unusual STYLE: '[Ellis Bell] had an inspiration which may yet find an audience in the outer world'. Only 20 of her poems were printed; most of Emily's poems were not published until the 20th century. She was influenced by Shelley, but her style and vision are unique, as they are in her one novel, *Wuthering Heights* (1847).

Like her sisters, Emily died tragically young, killed by tuberculosis. Her favourite dog, Keeper, howled outside her room for many days. She was, said Charlotte,

> rooted up in the prime of her days ... in the promise of her powers ... her existence now lies like a field of green corn trodden down, like a tree in full bearing struck at the root.

Long neglect

This poem describes an old portrait miniature.

Long neglect has worn away
Half the sweet enchanting smile
Time has turned the bloom to grey
Mould and damp the face defile[1]

But that lock[2] of silky hair
Still beneath the picture twined
Tells what once those features were
Paints their image on the mind

Fair the hand that traced[3] that line
'Dearest ever deem[4] me true'
Swiftly flew the fingers fine
When the pen that motto[5] drew

[1] make dirty [2] bunch [3] wrote [4] judge [5] short saying

What is the face like now? What was it once?
What is sad about the message?
What does the poem tell us about life and love?

W Write about an old object that you find, which belongs to someone who has died. What does the object tell you about the dead person, and how does it make you feel?

Emily and Anne kept many pets. Emily was a skilled artist and drew a fine sketch of her tame hawk, Hero. She saw such wild birds as SYMBOLS of her own nature.

And like myself

And like myself lone wholly lone[1]
It sees the day's long sunshine glow
And like myself it makes its moan[2]
In unexhausted woe[3]

Give we the hills our equal prayer
Earth's breezy hills and heaven's blue sea
We ask for nothing further here
But our own hearts and liberty

Ah could my hand unlock its chain
How gladly would I watch it soar[4]
And ne'er regret and ne'er complain
To see its shining eyes no more

But let me think that if today
It pines[5] in cold captivity
Tomorrow both shall soar away
Eternally entirely Free

[1] completely alone [2] feels sad [3] sorrow [4] fly up high
[5] wastes away

What similarities does Emily see between the bird and herself?
What do the poet and bird value most?
Why would she like to free the bird?
How will both of them eventually become free?
What does the bird seem to represent to the poet?

Emily Brontë, a true genius in an extraordinary family: portrait (about 1835) by her brother, Branwell.

The captive dove

Poor restless dove, I pity thee;
   And when I hear thy <u>plaintive moan</u>,[1]
I mourn for thy captivity,
   And in thy woes forget mine own.

To see thee stand prepared to fly,
   And flap those useless wings of thine,
And gaze into the distant sky,
   Would melt a harder heart than mine.

In vain – in vain! Thou canst not rise:
   Thy prison roof confines thee there;
Its slender wires <u>delude</u>[2] thine eyes,
   And <u>quench</u>[3] thy longings with despair.

Oh, thou were made to wander free
   In sunny <u>mead</u>[4] and shady grove,
And far beyond the rolling sea,
   In distant climes, at will to <u>rove</u>![5]

Yet, hadst thou but one gentle mate
   Thy little drooping heart to cheer,
And share with thee thy captive state,
   Thou couldst be happy even there.

Yes, even there, if, listening by,
   One faithful dear companion stood;
While gazing on her full bright eye,
   Thou might forget thy native wood.

But thou, poor solitary dove,
   Must make, unheard, thy joyless moan;
The heart that Nature formed to love
   Must pine, neglected, and alone.

Anne Brontë (1820-1849)

[1] sad sound   [2] trick   [3] stop   [4] meadow   [5] wander

D Compare the two poems above. Which is more powerful and why? What do Emily and Anne value most in life?

Remembrance

Cold in the earth – and the deep snow piled
                         above thee,
Far, far, removed, cold in the dreary grave!
Have I forgot, my only Love, to love thee,
<u>Severed</u>[1] at last by Time's all-severing wave?

Now, when alone, do my thoughts no longer
                           hover[2]
Over the mountains, on that <u>northern shore</u>,[3]
Resting their wings where heath and fern-leaves
                           cover
Thy noble heart for ever, ever more?

Cold in the earth – and fifteen wild Decembers,
From those brown hills, have melted into spring:
Faithful, indeed, is the spirit that remembers
After such years of change and suffering!

Emily and Anne Brontë writing their Gondal Saga
at Haworth Parsonage: the sisters' 'diary paper'
(1837).

Sweet Love of youth, forgive, if I forget thee,
While the world's tide is bearing me along;
Other desires and other hopes <u>beset</u>[4] me,
Hopes which <u>obscure</u>,[5] but cannot do thee wrong!

No later light has lightened up my heaven,
No second morn has ever shone for me;
All my life's bliss from thy dear life was given,
All my life's bliss is in the grave with thee.

But, when the days of golden dreams had
                         perished,[6]
And even Despair was powerless to destroy;
Then did I learn how existence could be
                         cherished,
Strengthened, and fed without the aid of joy.

Then did I <u>check</u>[7] the tears of useless passion –
<u>Weaned</u>[8] my young soul from <u>yearning after</u>[9] thine;
<u>Sternly denied</u>[10] its burning wish to hasten
Down to that tomb already more than mine.

And, even yet, I dare not let it <u>languish</u>,[11]
Dare not indulge in memory's <u>rapturous</u>[12] pain;
Once drinking deep of that <u>divinest anguish</u>,[13]
How could I seek the empty world again?

[1] cut off   [2] fly over   [3] (Angora, a kingdom in Gondal)
[4] attack   [5] hide you   [6] died   [7] stop   [8] gradually stopped
[9] longing for   [10] firmly refused   [11] lose strength
[12] ecstatic   [13] sweetest pain

This is a Gondal poem, a LAMENT for Julius Brenzaida, Prince of Angora, by Rosina, his wife. Into this fantasy, Emily poured an intense passion. Rhythm is one secret of its power. It is in PENTAMETER, but the first word is stressed and there is a heavy pause after the first two FEET in each line. Cecil Day Lewis, the poet, noted: 'It is the slowest rhythm I know and the most sombre'.

How does Emily Brontë use the seasons here?
What has happened to the speaker since the death?

What has not happened?
How has Rosina made herself strong?
What does she fear about remembrance?

W Write some entries in Rosina's journal, showing her thoughts about Julius and her own life at and since his death. Use plenty of ideas from the poem.

W How does Emily Brontë deal with regret, freedom and daydreams in her poems?

23 Elizabeth Barrett Browning (1806-1861): Not Death, but Love

After a wonderful childhood in a country house in Herefordshire, injury and illness turned Elizabeth Barrett into an invalid. When the family moved to Wimpole Street in London, she 'lay for years upon her back', confined to her room. Her father encouraged her to write, but refused to allow her any relationships with men: she would be guilty of 'unfilial treachery' if she married.

Her 1844 poetry collection won widespread praise. At this point Robert Browning first wrote to her: 'I do love these poems with all my heart – and I love you'. Their courtship began after his first visit and is movingly recorded in their letters and Elizabeth's SONNETS. Her health improved so much that, in 1846, she was able to slip out of Wimpole Street to marry Robert at a nearby church. They escaped to Italy and had a son in 1849. Elizabeth's subsequent poetry won her further praise, and Wordsworth even suggested that she should follow him as POET LAUREATE.

Elizabeth Barrett Browning took great interest in the many social problems of the Victorian era, and the poem *The cry of the children* (1844) had considerable impact. She read the Parliamentary reports on child labour in mines and factories. The use of workhouse orphans was particularly unpleasant, as they had no one to defend them. One such boy, Robert Blincoe, recalled the death of a girl in a machine:

> He saw her whirled round and round with the shaft – he heard the bones of her arms, legs and thighs snap asunder, crushed to atoms as the machinery whirled her round ... her blood was scattered over the frame, her head appeared dashed to pieces.

(*Memoir of Robert Blincoe*, 1832)

Child labour in the early Victorian era: illustration (1840) from Michael Armstrong, factory boy *by Fanny Trollope.*

from: **The cry of the children**

Do ye hear the children weeping, O my brothers,
        Ere[1] the sorrow comes with years?
They are leaning their young heads against their
                                mothers,
        And *that* cannot stop their tears.
The young lambs are bleating in the meadows,
    The young birds are chirping in the nest,
The young fawns[2] are playing with the shadows,
    The young flowers are blowing[3] toward the west –
But the young, young children, O my brothers,
        They are weeping bitterly!
They are weeping in the playtime of the others,
        In the country of the free.

They look up with their pale and sunken faces,
        And their looks are sad to see,
For the man's hoary anguish[4] draws and presses
        Down the cheeks of infancy.
'Your old earth,' they say, 'is very dreary;
    Our young feet,' they say, 'are very weak!
Few paces have we taken, yet are weary –
    Our grave-rest is very far to seek.
Ask the aged why they weep, and not the children;
        For the outside earth is cold;
And we young ones stand without,[5] in our
                                bewildering,
        And the graves are for the old.'

'True,' say the children, 'it may happen
        That we die before our time;
Little Alice died last year – her grave is shapen
        Like a snowball, in the rime.[6]
We looked into the pit prepared to take her:
    Was no room for any work in the close clay!
From the sleep wherein[7] she lieth none will
                                wake her,
    Crying, "Get up, little Alice! it is day."
If you listen by that grave, in sun and shower,
    With your ear down, little Alice never cries;
Could we see her face, be sure we should not
                                know her,
    For the smile has time for growing in her eyes:
And merry go her moments, lulled and stilled in
        The shroud[8] by the kirk-chime.[9]
'It is good when it happens,' say the children,
    'That we die before our time.'

'For oh,' say the children, 'we are weary,
        And we cannot run or leap;
If we cared for any meadows, it were merely
        To drop down in them and sleep.
Our knees tremble sorely in the stooping,
    We fall upon our faces, trying to go;
And, underneath our heavy eyelids drooping,
    The reddest flower would look as pale as snow;
For, all day, we drag our burden tiring
        Through the coal-dark, underground –
Or, all day, we drive the wheels of iron
        In the factories, round and round.

'For all day, the wheels are droning,[10] turning;
        Their wind comes in our faces, –
Till our hearts turn, – our heads with pulses
                                burning,
        And the walls turn in their places:
Turns the sky in the high window blank and
                                reeling,[11]
    Turns the long light that drops adown the wail,
Turn the black flies that crawl along the ceiling,
    All are turning, all the day, and we with all.
And all day, the iron wheels are droning,
        And sometimes we could pray,
"O ye wheels," (breaking out in a mad moaning)
        "Stop! be silent for to-day!" '

They look up with their pale and sunken faces,
        And their look is dread[12] to see,
For they mind you of their angels in high places,
        With eyes turned on Deity![13] –
'How long,' they say, 'how long, O cruel nation,
    Will you stand, to move the world, on a child's
                                heart, –
Stifle down[14] with a mailed[15] heel its palpitation,[16]
    And tread onward to your throne amid the mart?[17]
Our blood splashes upward, O gold-heaper,
        And your purple[18] shows your path!
But the child's sob in the silence curses deeper
        Than the strong man in his wrath![19]

[1] before [2] young deer [3] flowering [4] adult's pain
[5] outside [6] frost [7] in which [8] cloth covering a dead
body [9] church-bell [10] making a low, dull sound
[11] spinning round [12] terrible [13] God [14] crush
[15] covered with armour [16] irregular beating
[17] in the market [18] bloodstains [19] anger

Why is the **PHRASE** 'my brothers' used in the first
verse? To whom does it refer?
How does the poet use the ideas of youth and age in
the first two verses?
What is so terrible about the appearance of the
children in the second verse?
Why do the children envy 'little Alice'?
Why are the 'iron wheels' so frightening in the fourth
and fifth verses?
What message does the poet have for the nation?

W Write your own story or poem based on the
poem and the picture on page 61 from Fanny
Trollope's novel *Michael Armstrong, Factory Boy* (1840).

Sonnets From the Portuguese (1850) pretended
to be translations, but were actually a record of
Elizabeth's feelings during Robert's courtship of
her. The poems were composed in secret and only
shown to him three years after their marriage. The
first sonnet records her escape from imprisonment
in the home and illness into a full life when she
chose 'Not Death, but Love'.

Sonnet 24

Let the world's sharpness like a clasping knife
Shut in upon itself and do no harm
In this close hand of Love, now soft and warm,
And let us hear no sound of human strife[1]
After the click of the shutting. Life to life –
I lean upon thee, Dear, without alarm,
And feel as safe as guarded by a charm
Against the stab of worldlings,[2] who if rife[3]
Are weak to injure. Very whitely still
The lilies of our lives may reassure
Their blossoms from their roots, accessible
Alone to heavenly dews that drop not fewer:
Growing straight, out of man's reach, on the hill.
God only, who made us rich, can make us poor.

[1] struggling [2] people who are not spiritual [3] very common

Love is like a hand that shuts up a dangerous penknife.
Can you explain the comparison being made here? (The
continuation of the idea in 'the stab of worldlings'
might help you.)
How does the poet feel about her future husband in
the sentence starting 'Life to life'?
In the last six lines, the comparison changes. To what is
their love compared? Follow the details.
What is the summing up message of the last line?

W Explain the comparisons in this sonnet.

To the Brownings, love was not just a
relationship, but an intense joining of two people,
the most important and exciting experience in life:
'I love thee to the depth and breadth and
height/My soul can reach' (*Sonnet 43*). This
explains why Amy's cruelty is not cruelty at all.

Amy's cruelty

1

Fair Amy of the terraced house,
    Assist me to discover
Why you who would not hurt a mouse
    Can torture so your lover.

2

You give your coffee to the cat,
    You stroke the dog for coming,
And all your face grows kinder at
    The little brown bee's humming.

3

But when *he* haunts your door .. the town
    Marks coming and marks going ..
You seem to have stitched your eyelids down
    To that long piece of sewing!

4

You never give a look, not you,
    Nor drop him a 'Good-morning,'
To keep his long day warm and blue,
    So fretted[1] by your scorning.[2]

The close hand of love: Two lovers by a sundial
*(1870) by Arthur Hughes. [Ashmolean Museum,
University of Oxford]*

5

She shook her head – 'The mouse and bee
    For crumb or flower will linger:
The dog is happy at my knee,
    The cat purrs at my finger.

6

'But *he* .. to *him*, the least thing given
    Means great things at a distance;
He wants my world, my sun, my heaven,
    Soul, body, whole existence.

7

'They say love gives as well as takes;
    But I'm a simple maiden, –
My mother's first smile when she wakes
    I still have smiled and prayed in.

8

'I only know my mother's love
    Which gives all and asks nothing;
And this new loving sets the groove[3]
    Too much the way of loathing.[4]

9

'Unless he gives me all in change,[5]
    I forfeit all things by him:[6]
The risk is terrible and strange –
    I tremble, doubt, .. deny him.

10

'He's sweetest friend, or <u>hardest foe</u>,[7]
   Best angel, or worst devil;
I either hate or .. love him so,
   I can't be merely <u>civil</u>![8]

11

'You trust a woman who puts forth,
   Her blossoms thick as summer's?
You think she dreams what love is worth,
   Who <u>casts</u>[9] it to new-comers?

12

'Such love's a cowslip-ball to fling,
   A moment's pretty pastime;
I give .. all me, if anything,
   The first time and the last time.

13

'Dear neighbour of the trellised house,
   A man should murmur never,
Though treated worse than dog and mouse,
   Till <u>doted on</u>[10] for ever!'

(Last Poems, 1861)

[1] upset   [2] rejection   [3] fixes a path   [4] hating   [5] return
[6] give up everything for him   [7] worst enemy   [8] polite
[9] throws   [10] adored

What is pleasant about Amy? What seems to be unpleasant about her?
How does she compare the love of her mother to that of her lover?
What does she fear and resent about 'this new loving'?
What does she think of light-hearted, flirtatious love?
Why cannot Amy be 'merely civil'?
What sort of love does she want to give?
Imagine how Amy's lover feels about her behaviour. Does he understand it? Is he prepared to go on trying to get close to her?

D Role play a discussion with Amy about her so-called cruelty.

W Amy writes to a close friend, describing this conversation and her reactions to it. She makes clear her thoughts on love.

W How does Elizabeth Barrett Browning discuss public and private matters in these poems?

24 Robert Browning (1812-1889): Men and women

Born in Camberwell, then outside London, Browning was educated at home, where his father, a bank official, had collected a large library. Browning took Shelley as his model and decided early in life to be a poet. His first poems were criticised and he tried unsuccessfully to write plays. He then found his **STYLE** and method in *Dramatic LYRICS* (1842) and *Dramatic Romances* (1845). These attracted little notice, so that when he finally eloped to Italy in 1846, he was still only 'the man who married Elizabeth Barrett'.

Having settled in Florence, he found new subjects in Italian history for his vivid '**DRAMATIC MONOLOGUES**'. *Men and Women* (1855) was, he hoped, 'a first step towards popularity for me'. His characters were mostly from history, but his **THEME** was timeless: 'the corruption of the human heart'. Real fame only came to him with his 'Roman murder story', *The ring and the book* (1869), which turned him into a literary celebrity second only to Tennyson. He died in the palace he had bought in Venice.

Porphyria's lover

In Browning's dramatic monologues, 'utterances of so many imaginary persons, not mine', characters tell their stories by speaking their thoughts. This poem (1836) was an early success.

The rain set early in to-night,
   The sullen wind was soon awake,
It tore the elm-tops down for spite,
   And did its worst to <u>vex</u>[1] the lake:
   I listen'd with heart fit to break.
When glided in Porphyria; straight
   She shut the cold out and the storm,
And kneel'd and made the cheerless grate
   Blaze up, and all the cottage warm;
   Which done, she rose, and from her form
Withdrew the dripping cloak and shawl,
   And laid her soil'd gloves by, untied
Her hat and let the damp hair fall,
   And, last, she sat down by my side
   And call'd me. When no voice replied,
She put my arm about her waist,
   And made her smooth white shoulder bare,
And all her yellow hair <u>displaced</u>,[2]

And, stooping, made my cheek lie there,
    And spread, o'er all, her yellow hair,
Murmuring how she loved me – she
    Too weak, for all her heart's endeavour,[3]
To set its struggling passion free
    From pride, and vainer ties dissever,[4]
    And give herself to me for ever.
But passion sometimes would prevail,[5]
    Nor could to-night's gay[6] feast restrain[7]
A sudden thought of one so pale
    For love of her, and all in vain:
    So, she was come through wind and rain.
Be sure I look'd up at her eyes
    Happy and proud; at last I knew
Porphyria worshipp'd me; surprise
    Made my heart swell, and still it grew
    While I debated what to do.
That moment she was mine, mine, fair,
    Perfectly pure and good. I found
A thing to do, and all her hair
    In one long yellow string I wound
    Three times her little throat around,
And strangled her. No pain felt she;
    I am quite sure she felt no pain.
As a shut bud that holds a bee,
    I warily oped[8] her lids: again
    Laugh'd the blue eyes without a stain.
And I untighten'd next the tress
    About her neck; her cheek once more
Blush'd bright beneath my burning kiss:
    I propp'd her head up as before,
    Only, this time my shoulder bore[9]
Her head, which droops upon it still:
    The smiling rosy little head,
So glad it has its utmost will,
    That all it scorn'd[10] at once is fled,[11]
    And I, its love, am gain'd instead!
Porphyria's love: she guess'd not how
    Her darling one wish would be heard.
And thus we sit together now,
    And all night long we have not stirr'd,
And yet God has not said a word!

[1] disturb [2] loosed [3] efforts [4] break off [5] win [6] happy
[7] hold back [8] cautiously opened [9] supported
[10] rejected [11] gone

The poem starts with the young man alone in his cottage. How does the evening weather reflect his state of mind?
What effects does Porphyria's arrival have on the cottage and the man's mood?
Porphyria seems to live in a great house nearby where there is a 'gay feast', which she leaves to visit the speaker. What details does the poem give about Porphyria? What does she look like, how does she behave, and how does she treat the man?
Why has she come?
Just for a moment the man believes that Porphyria does love him. How does he react to this?
Which half-line is most shocking?
Can you understand why he kills her?
The poem was originally headed *Mad house cell*. How does the speaker show his madness and when do we see his insanity?
What does he do with the dead woman?
What is the impact of the last line?

W You are one of Porphyria's friends. Tell the story of Porphyria and her lover in a letter written after the murder.

D Role play an interview with Porphyria's lover.

Meeting at night

The grey sea and the long black land;
And the yellow half-moon large and low;
And the startled little waves that leap
In fiery ringlets from their sleep,
As I gain the cove with pushing prow,
And quench its speed in the slushy sand.

Then a mile of warm sea-scented beach;
Three fields to cross till a farm appears;
A tap at the pane, the quick sharp scratch
And blue spurt of a lighted match,
And a voice less loud, through its joys and fears,
Than the two hearts beating each to each!

Parting at morning

Round the cape of a sudden came the sea,
And the sun looked over the mountain's rim –
And straight was a path of gold for him,
And the need of a world of men for me.

These two linked poems tell a love story through hints and background, rather than through pictures of the lovers themselves.

Work out the setting of this romance, and the details of the journey that the man makes to see the woman.
Which words describing the setting also suggest the growing excitement of the man?
How is the woman described?
What does 'joys and fears' suggest about the relationship?
Parting is like an **AUBADE**. The man feels happy, strengthened and ready to face the world. How is this conveyed through the image of the rising sun?

W Write the full story of the lovers.

My last Duchess

That's my last Duchess painted on the wall,
Looking as if she were alive. I call
That piece a wonder, now: Frà Pandolf's hands
Worked busily a day, and there she stands.
Will 't please you sit and look at her? I said
'Frà Pandolf' by design, for never read
Strangers like you that pictured countenance,[1]
The depth and passion of its earnest glance,
But to myself they turned (since none puts by[2]
The curtain I have drawn for you, but I)
And seemed as they would ask me, if they durst,[3]
How such a glance came there; so, not the first
Are you to turn and ask thus. Sir, 't was not
Her husband's presence only, called that spot
Of joy into the Duchess' cheek: perhaps
Frà Pandolf chanced to say 'Her mantle laps[4]
Over my lady's wrist too much,' or 'Paint
Must never hope to reproduce the faint
Half-flush that dies along her throat:' such stuff
Was courtesy, she thought, and cause enough
For calling up that spot of joy. She had
A heart – how shall I say? – too soon made glad,
Too easily impressed; she liked whate'er
She looked on, and her looks went everywhere.
Sir, 't was all one! My favour[5] at her breast,
The dropping of the daylight in the West,

The bough of cherries some officious[6] fool
Broke in the orchard for her, the white mule
She rode with round the terrace – all and each
Would draw from her alike the approving speech,
Or blush, at least. She thanked men, – good! but
        thanked
Somehow – I know not how – as if she ranked
My gift of a nine-hundred-years-old name[7]
With anybody's gift. Who'd stoop to blame
This sort of trifling? Even had you skill
In speech – (which I have not) – to make your will
Quite clear to such an one, and say, 'Just this
Or that in you disgusts me; here you miss,
Or there exceed the mark' – and if she let
Herself be lessoned so, nor plainly set
Her wits to yours, forsooth[8], and made excuse,
– E'en then would be some stooping; and I choose
Never to stoop. Oh sir, she smiled, no doubt,
Whene'er I passed her; but who passed without
Much the same smile? This grew; I gave commands;
Then all smiles stopped together. There she stands
As if alive. Will 't please you rise? We'll meet
The company below, then. I repeat,
The Count your master's known munificence[9]
Is ample warrant[10] that no just pretence[11]
Of mine for dowry[12] will be disallowed;
Though his fair daughter's self, as I avowed[13]
At starting, is my object. Nay, we'll go
Together down, sir. Notice Neptune, though,
Taming a sea-horse, thought a rarity,
Which Claus of Innsbruck cast in bronze for me!

[1] face   [2] pulls back   [3] dared   [4] cloak falls   [5] love token
[6] self-important   [7] (of the Este family)   [8] argued, indeed
[9] generosity   [10] more than enough guarantee   [11] rightful
claim   [12] money given with the bride   [13] stated

Alfonso, Duke of Ferrara (1537-1597), from the powerful Este family, married 14-year-old Lucrezia de Medici in 1558. Three years later she was dead, probably poisoned. The Duke then married the daughter of the Count of Tyrol, whose capital was Innsbruck. The marriage arrangements were made by a representative.

How does the Duke treat the portrait of his wife?
What did he dislike about his wife's behaviour?
Why was he so jealous of her?
What impression do you get of the young wife?
Why did the Duke not tell her how he felt?
What does the phrase 'I gave commands' suggest?
What is the Duke's main concern in negotiating for a new bride?
Does the Duke like possessions better than people?

W Write the envoy's report about his meeting with the Duke for his master in Innsbruck.

W Write about the various and surprising ways that Browning deals with the theme of love.

The Duke shows the Austrian envoy his bronze sea-horse: Victorian illustration for My last Duchess.

25 Matthew Arnold (1822-1888): The strange disease of modern life

Arnold was an uneasy figure; he felt himself to be 'wandering between two worlds,/One dead, the other powerless to be born'. His father was a famous reforming headmaster of Rugby School, which Arnold went to before going to Oxford University.

Needing a regular income to marry, he became a school inspector. The church elementary schools he saw were often depressingly poor and his district was huge, involving him in exhausting travel. His first child was born, he recalled, in Derby lodgings with a workhouse in front and a prison behind. He spoke out bravely against the government's 'payment by results' system of managing schools, and campaigned for state secondary schooling.

Arnold published several books of poems in the 1850s and 1860s. He often used German and Greek models and portrayed the alienation and materialism of his time:

> This strange disease of modern life,
> With its sick hurry, its divided aims,
> Its heads o'ertaxed ...

> (from: *The Scholar Gypsy*)

'The nightingales divinely sing': illustration (1900) for To Marguerite.

The uncertainty of the mid-Victorian era seemed to affect relationships too. Here are two poems on loneliness and love.

To Marguerite

Yes! in the sea of life enisled,[1]
With echoing straits[2] between us thrown,
Dotting the shoreless watery wild,
We mortal millions live *alone*.
The islands feel the enclasping flow,
And then their endless bounds[3] they know.

But when the moon their hollows lights,
And they are swept by balms[4] of spring,
And in their glens, on starry nights,
The nightingales divinely sing;
And lovely notes, from shore to shore,
Across the sounds[5] and channels pour –

Oh! then a longing like despair
Is to their farthest caverns sent;
For surely once, they feel, we were
Parts of a single continent!
Now round us spreads the watery plain –
Oh might our marges[6] meet again!

Who order'd, that their longing's fire
Should be, as soon as kindled, cool'd?
Who renders vain[7] their deep desire? –
A God, a God their severance[8] ruled!
And bade[9] betwixt their shores to be
The unplumb'd,[10] salt, estranging[11] sea.

[1] made into an island [2] narrow channels of sea [3] limits [4] sweet smells [5] channels of sea [6] edges [7] makes pointless [8] separation [9] ordered [10] so deep it has not been measured [11] alienating

Too late

Each on his own strict line we move,
And some find death ere[1] they find love;
So far apart their lives are thrown
From the twin soul which halves their own.

And sometimes, by still harder fate,
The lovers meet, but meet too late.
– Thy heart is mine! – *True, true! ah, true!*
– Then, love, thy hand! – *Ah no! adieu![2]*

[1] before [2] goodbye

Marguerite was a Swiss woman whom Arnold briefly loved. He wrote the first poem when they parted. He was becoming convinced that real relationships were becoming impossible in the 'rush and glare' of modern life.

What comparisons are used to describe human isolation in each poem?

Why is love frustrating, as it is shown here?

D What is the message of each poem? Do you think people are as isolated as Arnold makes out?

Dover beach

The sea is calm to-night.
The tide is full, the moon lies fair
Upon the straits; – on the French coast the light
Gleams and is gone; the cliffs of England stand,
Glimmering and vast, out in the tranquil bay.
Come to the window, sweet is the night-air!

Only, from the long line of spray
Where the sea meets the moon-blanch'd[1] land,
Listen! you hear the grating roar
Of pebbles which the waves draw back, and fling,
At their return, up the high strand,[2]
Begin, and cease, and then again begin,
With tremulous cadence[3] slow, and bring
The eternal note of sadness in.

Sophocles[4] long ago
Heard it on the Ægæan,[5] and it brought
Into his mind the turbid[6] ebb and flow
Of human misery; we
Find also in the sound a thought,
Hearing it by this distant northern sea.

The Sea of Faith
Was once, too, at the full, and round earth's shore
Lay like the folds of a bright girdle furl'd.[7]
But now I only hear
Its melancholy, long, withdrawing roar,
Retreating, to the breath
Of the night-wind, down the vast edges drear
And naked shingles[8] of the world.

Ah, love, let us be true
To one another! for the world, which seems
To lie before us like a land of dreams,
So various, so beautiful, so new,
Hath really neither joy, nor love, nor light,
Nor certitude,[9] nor peace, nor help for pain;
And we are here as on a darkling[10] plain
Swept with confused alarms of struggle and flight,
Where ignorant armies clash by night.

[1] whitened [2] beach [3] slightly shaking rhythm
[4] (Arnold's favourite Greek dramatist) [5] sea near Greece
[6] disordered [7] folded belt [8] beaches [9] something not
to be doubted [10] nearly dark

This poem reflects Arnold's and society's loss of religious faith.

Which words create the quiet mood of the opening? Why is there 'The eternal note of sadness' in the sound of the sea? What did Sophocles think of the sound of waves? How does Arnold move the idea from the sea to Christian faith in the fourth verse?

Matthew Arnold, poet and school inspector: portrait (1855) by G. F. Watts.

Which lines sum up what is happening to faith? Without religion, there is only one sure value left; what is it?

W Write a detailed discussion of the meaning and language of this poem.

The great Victorians were determined reformers and believers in progress. Arnold wrote these lines about his father, reminded of him Thomas Hughes's *Tom Brown's Schooldays* (1857), which praised the great headmaster.

from: Rugby chapel

What is the course of the life
Of mortal men on the earth? –
Most men eddy[1] about
Here and there – eat and drink,
Chatter and love and hate,
Gather and squander,[2] are raised
Aloft,[3] are hurl'd in the dust,
Striving[4] blindly, achieving
Nothing; and then they die –
Perish; – and no one asks
Who or what they have been,
More than he asks what waves,
In the moonlit solitudes mild
Of the midmost Ocean, have swell'd,
Foam'd for a moment, and gone.

And there are some, whom a thirst
Ardent, unquenchable,[5] fires,
Not with the crowd to be spent,
Not without aim to go round
In an eddy of purposeless dust,
Effort unmeaning and vain.
Ah yes! some of us strive
Not without action to die
Fruitless, but something to snatch
From dull oblivion,[6] nor all
Glut[7] the devouring grave!
We, we have chosen our path –
Path to a clear-purposed goal,
Path of advance!

[1] swirl   [2] waste   [3] up high   [4] struggling   [5] burning, that cannot be satisfied   [6] state of being completely forgotten   [7] stuff

How do most men live?
What vivid comparison is used to describe most human lives?
What is different about the great reformers? What ambitions do they have?

D Discuss the optimism and pessimism about human life presented in these poems.

26 Christina Rossetti (1830-1894): Heart-broken for a little love

Christina's father was an exiled Italian radical who taught at the new London University. Her mother educated Christina well at home, proudly keeping a record of her writing: Christina's first poems were published when she was only 12.

Her brothers, William and Dante Gabriel, an artist and writer, founded the Pre-Raphaelite Brotherhood, a circle of artists who imitated the brightly coloured, boldly detailed work of Italian artists before Raphael (1483-1520). Christina posed for Dante and her face appears in several Pre-Raphaelite paintings. Her poetry, with its bright colours and details, often resembles Pre-Raphaelite work. Several of her poems appeared in the circle's magazine, *The Germ*, in 1850.

Christina's life had few events. She stayed in the family, living mostly in London. Illness made her increasingly housebound. Two engagements were broken off, giving a possible reason for her many poems of frustrated or unhappy love. She herself denied that her poems were 'love personals'. That style of 'mournful verse', with its 'broken betrayal MOTIF', was common in Victorian women's poetry.

Goblin Market (1862), a powerful fantasy poem about the clash of innocence and experience, was Christina's most remarkable work, and *The Prince's Progress* (1866) was her other major collection. Her brother William noted that 'her habits of composition were entirely of the casual and spontaneous'. This was the Victorian male idea of the female poet, whose words were supposed to come from the heart and not the head. In fact,

Christina composed very carefully. In later life she turned entirely to religious writing; her beautiful carol *In the bleak mid-winter* (1871) remains a favourite.

Christina Rossetti: one of many portraits of her by her brother, the artist and poet, Dante Gabriel Rossetti.

Cousin Kate

I was a cottage maiden
  Hardened by sun and air,
Contented with my cottage mates,
  Not mindful[1] I was fair.
Why did a great lord find me out,
  And praise my flaxen[2] hair?
Why did a great lord find me out
  To fill my heart with care?

He lured[3] me to his palace home –
  Woe's me for joy thereof[4] –
To lead a shameless shameful life,
  His plaything and his love.
He wore me like a silken knot,
  He changed me like a glove;
So now I moan, an unclean thing,
  Who might have been a dove.

O Lady Kate, my cousin Kate,
  You grew more fair than I:
He saw you at your father's gate,
  Chose you, and cast me by.[5]
He watched your steps along the lane,
  Your work among the rye;
He lifted you from mean estate[6]
  To sit with him on high.

Because you were so good and pure
  He bound[7] you with his ring:
The neighbours call you good and pure,
  Call me an outcast[8] thing.
Even so I sit and howl in dust,
  You sit in gold and sing:
Now which of us has tenderer heart?
  You had the stronger wing.

O cousin Kate, my love was true,
  Your love was writ in sand:
If he had fooled not me but you,
  If you stood where I stand,
He'd not have won me with his love
  Nor bought me with his land;
I would have spit into his face
  And not have taken his hand.

Yet I've a gift you have not got,
  And seem not like to get:
For all your clothes and wedding-ring
  I've little doubt you fret.[9]
My fair-haired son, my shame, my pride,
  Cling closer, closer yet:
Your father would give lands for one
  To wear his coronet.[10]

[1] realising [2] soft yellow [3] attracted [4] I'm sad now
because I was happy there [5] got rid of me [6] humble
rank [7] tied [8] rejected [9] worry [10] crown

This is one of several attractive **BALLAD**-like
poems about women who are rivals in love. It may
have been influenced by Christina's experiences
when she did voluntary work at a London Reform
Home for young prostitutes.

The original title of this poem was *Up and down.*
Which is better?
What is the story of the **NARRATOR**?
What comparisons are used to show the man's
treatment of her?
What is the story of Kate? What did she achieve that
the narrator did not?
What does 'You sit in gold and sing' mean?
How would the narrator have behaved if the lord had
cheated Kate?
What is the twist in the last verse?
Why is the child 'my shame, my pride'? Why should he
'cling closer'?

W Write this story as a prose **NARRATIVE** in your
own words. You could use the viewpoints of the
narrator, Kate, and the lord.

L. E. L.

'Whose heart was breaking for a little love.'

Downstairs I laugh, I sport and jest[1] with all:
  But in my solitary room above
I turn my face in silence to the wall;
  My heart is breaking for a little love.
    Tho' winter frosts are done,
    And birds pair every one,
And leaves peep out, for springtide is begun.

I feel no spring, while spring is wellnigh blown,[2]
  I find no nest, while nests are in the grove:
Woe's me[3] for mine own heart that dwells alone,
  My heart that breaketh for a little love.
    While golden in the sun
    Rivulets[4] rise and run,
While lilies bud, for springtide is begun.

All love, are loved, save only I;[5] their hearts
  Beat warm with love and joy, beat full thereof:[6]
They cannot guess, who play the pleasant parts,
  My heart is breaking for a little love.
    While beehives wake and whirr,
    And rabbit thins his fur,
In living spring that sets the world astir.[7]

I deck[8] myself with silks and jewelry,
  I plume myself like any mated dove:
They praise my rustling show, and never see
  My heart is breaking for a little love.
    While sprouts green lavender
    With rosemary and myrrh,[9]
For in quick[10] spring the sap is all astir.

Perhaps some saints in glory guess the truth,
  Perhaps some angels read it as they move,
And cry one to another full of ruth,[11]
  'Her heart is breaking for a little love.'
    Tho' other things have birth,
    And leap and sing for mirth,[12]
When springtime wakes and clothes and feeds
                              the earth.

'My heart is like a singing bird': Love (1856)
by John Everett Millais, a Pre-Raphaelite painter.

Yet saith a saint: 'Take patience for thy scathe;'[13]
   Yet saith an angel: 'Wait, for thou shalt prove
True best is last, true life is born of death,
   O thou, heart-broken for a little love.
      Then love shall fill thy girth,[14]
      And love make fat thy dearth,[15]
When new spring builds new heaven and clean
                              new earth.'

[1] play and joke [2] nearly at its peak [3] I am sad
[4] small streams [5] except for me [6] of it [7] in motion
[8] dress [9] a sweet-smelling plant [10] full of life [11] pity
[12] happiness [13] injury [14] body [15] lack

   L. E. L. was Letitia E. Landon (1802-1838), a
pioneer woman poet, much admired by later 19th-
century women writers. She killed herself after a
brief, unhappy marriage. Elizabeth Barrett
Browning wrote a poem about her and saw her as
'one thirsty for a little love'. Christina writes more
indirectly about unhappiness in love.

How does the woman behave in public and in private?
What details does she give of fertility in the natural
world? How do these details contrast with herself?
What religious consolation does she find?

A birthday

By contrast, this poem is about happy love.

My heart is like a singing bird
   Whose nest is in a watered shoot;[1]
My heart is like an apple tree
   Whose boughs are bent with thickset fruit;
My heart is like a rainbow shell
   That paddles in a halcyon[2] sea;
My heart is gladder than all these
   Because my love is come to me.

Raise me a dais[3] of silk and down;
   Hang it with vair[4] and purple dyes;
Carve it in doves and pomegranates,
   And peacocks with a hundred eyes;
Work it in gold and silver grapes,
   In leaves and silver fleurs-de-lys;[5]
Because the birthday of my life
   Is come, my love is come to me.

[1] young tree [2] calm [3] platform [4] fur [5] lilies

Why is the poem called *A birthday*?
How does the poet use beautiful things in nature to
reflect her mood?
Why mention the exotic decorations in verse two?

W Contrast these two poems about love. What is
the mood of each and how does each use the
background to reflect state of mind?

Noble sisters

'Now did you mark[1] a falcon,
   Sister dear, sister dear,
Flying toward my window
   In the morning cool and clear?
With jingling bells about her neck,
   But what beneath her wing?
It may have been a ribbon,
   Or it may have been a ring.' –
   'I marked a falcon swooping
      At the break of day:
   And for your love, my sister dove,
      I frayed[2] the thief away.' –

'Or did you spy[3] a ruddy[4] hound,
   Sister fair and tall,
Went snuffing round my garden bound,
   Or crouched by my bower[5] wall?
With a silken leash about his neck;
   But in his mouth may be
A chain of gold and silver links,
   Or a letter writ to me.' –
   'I heard a hound, highborn sister,
      Stood baying[6] at the moon:
   I rose and drove him from your wall
      Lest you should wake too soon.' –

'Or did you meet a pretty page[7]
  Sat swinging on the gate;
Sat whistling like a bird,
  Or may be slept too late:
With eaglets broidered[8] on his cap,
  And eaglets on his glove?
If you had turned his pockets out,
  You had found some pledge[9] of love.' –
  'I met him at this daybreak,
    Scarce the east was red:
  Lest the creaking gate should anger you,
    I packed him home to bed.' –

'Oh patience, sister. Did you see
  A young man tall and strong,
Swift-footed to uphold the right
  And to uproot the wrong,
Come home across the desolate[10] sea
  To woo me for his wife?
And in his heart my heart is locked,
  And in his life my life.' –
  'I met a nameless man, sister,
    Who loitered[11] round our door:
  I said: Her husband loves her much,
    And yet she loves him more.' –

'Fie,[12] sister, fie, a wicked lie,
  A lie, a wicked lie,
I have none other love but him,
  Nor will have till I die.
And you have turned him from our door,
  And stabbed him with a lie:
I will go seek him thro' the world
  In sorrow till I die.' –

'Go seek in sorrow, sister,
  And find in sorrow too:
If thus you shame our father's name
  My curse go forth with you.'

[1] notice [2] frightened [3] see [4] reddish [5] summerhouse
[6] howling [7] young servant of a knight [8] embroidered
[9] promise [10] deserted, gloomy [11] hung around [12] oh no

Like many Victorian poets, Christina Rossetti enjoyed writing medieval fantasy stories. She used the old ballad style of story-telling, of which **DIALOGUE** is a common feature.

What messengers has the young man used to reach his love in the first three verses?
What has the second sister done to the messengers?
What do we learn in the fourth verse about the young man who courts the first young woman?
What story has the second sister told the young man to get rid of him?
Why has the second sister acted so harshly throughout?
Look at the little pictures that are built up in the first four lines of the first four verses. How effective do you think the details are?

W Tell the full story of the first sister's love for the young man, and the reasons for her sister's jealousy. Say what happens next in the story.

D In pairs practise reading this poem aloud.

27 Gerard Manley Hopkins (1844-1889): Beauty and God

In his journal, which he began as a student at Oxford University, Hopkins recorded the two key influences on his ideas. Firstly, his tutor, Walter Pater (1839-1894), taught him that appreciation of beauty was life's greatest experience. Hopkins kept a 'treasury of explored beauty' in his journal:

August 30 1867: Putting my hand up against the sky whilst we lay on the grass I saw more richness and beauty in the blue than I had ever known before ... turquoise-like, swarming and blushing round the edge of the hand.

Hopkins developed a theory of individual patterns and shapes in all natural objects, which he called 'inscape'. Secondly, he was affected by the Oxford Movement, which wanted to take the Church of England closer to Catholicism. In a painful break with his family, he became a Catholic and eventually joined the strict Jesuit Order as a priest.

He then destroyed his early poems, resolving 'to give up all beauty until I had His leave for it'. In 1875, however, the deaths of some Catholic nuns in a shipwreck made him write again in his fresh, experimental **STYLE**. Other poems followed, especially during a happy time at a college in Wales. His **THEME** was often the beauty of the world as an expression of God. Only friends saw the poems, this freedom from a public audience allowing him to experiment with his word **COINAGES** and **SPRUNG RHYTHM**.

He found his work as priest and teacher difficult. His final post as Professor of Greek at Dublin University exhausted him and he died prematurely of typhoid fever in 1889. Hopkins's collected poems were not published until 1918.

Spring

Nothing is so beautiful as spring –
   When weeds, in wheels, shoot long and lovely
                        and lush;[1]
   Thrush's eggs look little low heavens, and thrush
Through the echoing timber does so rinse and
                        wring
The ear, it strikes like lightnings to hear him sing;
   The glassy peartree leaves and blooms, they brush
   The descending blue; that blue is all in a rush
With richness; the racing lambs too have fair
                        their fling.

What is all this juice and all this joy?
   A strain[2] of the earth's sweet being in the
                        beginning
In Eden garden. – Have, get, before it cloy,[3]
   Before it cloud, Christ, lord, and sour with
                        sinning,
Innocent mind and Mayday in girl and boy,
   Most, O maid's child, thy choice and worthy
                        the winning.

[1] growing thickly and strongly   [2] surviving part of
[3] grows tired

'Thrush's eggs' look like miniature skies. Why is the comparison a good one?
'Rinse' and 'wring' are words taken from the washing process. Why are they suitable in a description of hearing birdsong?

Gerard Manley Hopkins, the Jesuit priest, photographed in 1880.

The detail of the tree and sky are taken from Hopkins's journal, quoted above. Can you understand 'descending'? Of what does the spring remind the poet? What religious message is attached to the vivid description of spring?

Hopkins returned to Oxford as a priest in 1878. The felling of a line of poplars at Binsey near Godstow made him feel as if part of his youth had gone. The use of the wood in brake blocks for steam engines further upset him: the railway was going to destroy England's beauty.

Binsey poplars

Felled 1879

   My aspens dear, whose airy cages quelled,[1]
   Quelled or quenched in leaves the leaping sun,
   All felled, felled, are all felled;
      Of a fresh and following folded rank
           Not spared, not one
           That dandled a sandalled
        Shadow that swam or sank
On meadow and river and wind-wandering
   weed-winding bank.

   O if we but knew what we do
        When we delve or hew[2] –
   Hack and rack the growing green!
        Since country is so tender
   To touch, her being so slender,
   That, like this sleek and seeing ball
   But a prick will make no eye at all,
   Where we, even where we mean
          To mend her we end her,
      When we hew or delve:
After-comers cannot guess the beauty been.
   Ten or twelve, only ten or twelve
      Strokes of havoc[3] unselve
        The sweet especial scene,
      Rural scene, a rural scene,
      Sweet especial rural scene.

[1] overcame   [2] dig or cut   [3] destruction

The trees are remembered through comparisons. Explain each one, looking at 'cages' and 'sandalled' especially.
What beautiful details are given of the river scene?
How well do you think the **ALLITERATION** and **INTERNAL RHYMES** work in the opening verse? What effects are they trying to create?
How is the cutting down of the trees related to the human eye?
Do you find the conclusion convincing or sentimental?

D   Many people get very angry when trees that they love are threatened. What do trees stand for? Why do people have such strong feelings about them?

Spring and fall
To a young child

Margaret, are you grieving
Over Goldengrove unleaving?
Leaves, like the things of man, you
With your fresh thoughts care for, can you?
Ah! as the heart grows older
It will come to such sights colder
By and by, nor spare a sigh
Though worlds of wanwood leafmeal lie;
And yet you will weep and know why,
Now no matter, child, the name:
Sorrow's springs are the same.
Nor mouth had, no nor mind, expressed
What heart heard of, ghost[1] guessed:
It is the blight[2] man was born for,
It is Margaret you mourn for.

[1] soul   [2] curse

In September 1880 Hopkins sent this poem to a
friend. In it he imagines a child watching leaves fall.
She cannot explain why she is sad about them. It is
a feeling from the 'heart' or 'ghost', not the mind.

What answer does the poet offer Margaret?
What is the 'blight man was born for'?
What do you think the coinages 'leafmeal' and
'wanwood' mean? Why has the poet invented these
words?

W   How does Hopkins write about nature and
people?

Read the poem below from *A Shropshire Lad* by A. E.
Housman (1859-1936).

Loveliest of trees

Loveliest of trees, the cherry now
Is hung with bloom along the bough,
And stands about the woodland ride[1]
Wearing white for Eastertide.

Now, of my threescore years and ten,[2]
Twenty will not come again,
And take from seventy springs a score,
It only leaves me fifty more.

And since to look at things in bloom
Fifty springs are little room,
About the woodlands I will go
To see the cherry hung with snow.

[1] path   [2] (a score is 20. In the Bible (Psalm 90: 10), it says
that people live for 70 years)

D   Compare Hopkins's autumn poem with
Housman's similarly thoughtful spring picture. Explain
what both poems say about trees, people, time and
death.

•PART 6•
Late nineteenth- and early twentieth-century poetry

28 Thomas Hardy (1840-1928): Poems from two centuries

Hardy, son of a stonemason, was the famous author of such novels as *Far from the Madding Crowd* (1874) or *Tess of the d'Urbervilles* (1891); they are set in his native Dorset countryside. After *Jude the Obscure* (1896), he gave up the novel and published only poems. Time, change and memory were his favourite **THEMES**.

Hardy met his future wife, Emma Gifford, in Cornwall in March 1870. Their courtship that summer was very happy, as was their marriage when it began in 1874. It ended in bitterness and alienation. Emma died in 1912. In March 1913 Hardy revisited the West Country and the places of his courtship. The **ELEGIES** about Emma that resulted have been called 'some of the finest love poems – certainly love poems of married life – ever written'.

Emma Gifford, drawn by Hardy during their courtship in August 1870. She is trying to rescue a picnic glass lost in a stream.

The voice

Woman much missed, how you call to me, call to me,
Saying that now you are not as you were
When you had changed from the one who was
                       all to me,
But as at first, when our day was fair.

Can it be you that I hear? Let me view you, then,
Standing as when I drew near to the town
Where you would wait for me: yes, as I knew you
                       then,
Even to the original air-blue gown!

Or is it only the breeze, in its listlessness[1]
Travelling across the wet mead[2] to me here,
You being ever dissolved to wan[3] wistlessness[4]
Heard no more again far or near?

    Thus I; faltering[5] forward,
    Leaves around me falling,
Wind oozing thin through the thorn from norward,[6]
    And the woman calling.

[1] lack of energy   [2] meadow   [3] pale   [4] state of being forgotten   [5] moving uncertainly   [6] the north

What does Hardy think he hears Emma's voice saying?
What vivid detail does he remember about her in the second verse?
Then he doubts the voice. What might it be?
Why does the rhythm change change after the third verse? What new mood comes in?
What do the leaves, thorn and wind have to do with Hardy himself?
Why is the calling different in the last line?

W Write Hardy's diary entry about this haunting incident, including his memories and changes of mood.

During wind and rain

This poem was inspired by episodes in Emma Hardy's simple **AUTOBIOGRAPHY**, *Some Recollections*, which is about her Plymouth childhood.

> They sing their dearest songs –
> He, she, all of them – yea,
> Treble and tenor and bass,
>   And one to play;
> With the candles mooning each face ....
>   Ah, no; the years O!
> How the sick leaves reel[1] down in throngs!
>
> They clear the creeping moss –
> Elders and juniors – aye,
> Making the pathways neat
>   And the garden gay;[2]
> And they build a shady seat ....
>   Ah, no; the years, the years;
> See, the white storm-birds wing across.
>
> They are blithely[3] breakfasting all –
> Men and maidens – yea,
> Under the summer tree,
>   With a glimpse of the bay,
> While pet fowl[4] come to the knee ....
>   Ah, no; the years O!
> And the rotten rose is ript from the wall.
>
> They change to a high new house,
> He, she, all of them – aye,
> Clocks and carpets and chairs
>   On the lawn all day,
> And brightest things that are theirs ....
>   Ah, no; the years, the years;
> Down their carved names the rain-drop ploughs.

[1] whirl   [2] bright   [3] happily   [4] birds

Each verse has a grim **REFRAIN**. The 'Ah!' and 'O!' that change the rhythm echo the folk music Hardy knew as a child. While the verses are in the past tense, the refrains are in the present.

The first five lines of each verse show a scene from the family's past. What are they doing in each memory picture?
What does each refrain tell us about time and change?
In the last line, what does the word 'ploughs' suggest that time and weather are doing to the names on the gravestones? What is the force of this?

W Write your own contrast piece, perhaps based on old photographs, showing the changes in a family from past to present. Alternatively, imagine revisiting in the future scenes that are familiar to you now.

The darkling[1] thrush

This poem was written in December 1900: its first title was *By the century's death bed*.

> I leant upon a coppice[2] gate
>   When frost was spectre-grey,[3]
> And Winter's dregs[4] made desolate
>   The weakening eye of day.
> The tangled bine-stems[5] scored[6] the sky
>   Like strings of broken lyres,[7]
> And all mankind that haunted nigh[8]
>   Had sought their household fires.
>
> The land's sharp features seemed to be
>   The Century's corpse outleant,[9]
> His crypt[10] the cloudy canopy,[11]
>   The wind his death-lament,
> The ancient pulse of germ[12] and birth
>   Was shrunken hard and dry,
> And every spirit upon earth
>   Seemed fervourless[13] as I.
>
> At once a voice arose among
>   The bleak twigs overhead
> In a full-hearted evensong[14]
>   Of joy illimited;[15]
> An aged thrush, frail, gaunt,[16] and small,
>   In blast-beruffled plume,[17]
> Had chosen thus to fling his soul
>   Upon the growing gloom.
>
> So little cause for carollings[18]
>   Of such ecstatic[19] sound
> Was written on terrestrial[20] things
>   Afar or nigh around,[21]
> That I could think there trembled through
>   His happy good-night air
> Some blessed Hope, whereof he knew[22]
>   And I was unaware.

[1] twilight   [2] small wood   [3] grey as a ghost   [4] remains   [5] climbing, twisting stems   [6] cut   [7] stringed musical instruments   [8] lived nearby   [9] lying stretched out   [10] tomb   [11] covering   [12] creation   [13] without energy   [14] evening hymn   [15] without limits   [16] weak, thin   [17] feathers   [18] songs   [19] joyful   [20] earthly   [21] far away or nearby   [22] which he knew about

To what is the landscape likened in the second verse?
The last two verses contrast sharply with the first two. Which words express the joy of the thrush's song?
Why does the bird seem an unlikely optimist?
What does the bird's message seem to be for the new century?

D Discuss some of the good and bad things about the 20th century. What do you think now about the thrush's 'blessed Hope'?

W Write your own piece about the end of the 20th century and the start of the 21st.

The Titanic *disaster of April 1912: illustration from* Sphere *magazine. Although supposedly unsinkable, the ship went down in two and a half hours on her maiden voyage to New York.*

The convergence[1] of the twain[2]

Hardy wrote this poem to help the Disaster Fund when the *Titanic* sank after hitting an iceberg in the Atlantic in 1912. More than 1,500 people died.

1

In a solitude of the sea
Deep from human vanity,[3]
And the Pride of Life[4] that planned her, stilly
couches[5] she.

2

Steel chambers, late[6] the pyres[7]
Of her salamandrine[8] fires,
Cold currents thrid[9] and turn to rhythmic tidal lyres.[10]

3

Over the mirrors meant
To glass the opulent[11]
The sea-worm crawls – grotesque,[12] slimed,
dumb, indifferent.[13]

4

Jewels in joy designed
To ravish the sensuous mind[14]
Lie lightless, all their sparkles bleared[15] and black
and blind.

5

Dim moon-eyed fishes near
Gaze at the gilded[16] gear
And query: 'What does this vaingloriousness[17]
down here?' ...

6

Well: while was fashioning[18]
This creature of cleaving[19] wing,
The Immanent Will that stirs and urges everything

7

Prepared a sinister[20] mate
For her – so gaily[21] great –
A Shape of Ice, for the time far and dissociate.[22]

8

And as the smart ship grew
In stature,[23] grace, and hue,[24]
In shadowy silent distance grew the Iceberg too.

9

Alien[25] they seemed to be:
No mortal eye could see
The intimate[26] welding of their later history,

10

Or sign that they were bent
By paths coincident[27]
On being anon[28] twin halves of one august[29] event,

11

Till the Spinner of the Years
Said 'Now!' And each one hears,
And consummation[30] comes, and jars[31] two
hemispheres.[32]

[1] coming together [2] two [3] pride [4] confident materialism [5] lies quietly [6] recently [7] place for burning the dead [8] where a fire creature might live [9] threaded [10] stringed musical instruments [11] rich [12] ugly and deformed [13] not caring [14] to give great delight to the senses [15] made dim [16] covered with gold [17] pride [18] being made [19] cutting [20] threatening [21] full of cheerful life [22] unconnected [23] size [24] colour [25] completely different [26] close [27] coming together [28] soon [29] very important [30] completion of the act (the collision) [31] jolts [32] two sides of the world (Europe and the USA)

Hardy believed in a grim God of Fate that guided and twisted human lives. Here it is called 'Immanent Will' and 'Spinner of the Years'.

Where is the ship in verses 1 to 5? Which aspects of it are described? What contrasts are made? Which impresses you most?
How did the ship represent 'vanity' and 'Pride of Life'?

Which **PHRASES** contrast the liner and the iceberg? Which make the two seem like lovers?

W After doing more research into the *Titanic*, write your own poem about the disaster.

W Newspapers at the time focused on 'human stories': the orchestra that played to the end; the captain's last message – 'Be British'. Write such an article.

29 D. H. Lawrence (1885-1930): Harmony and discord

Lawrence is best known as the author of *Sons and Lovers* (1913) and *The Rainbow* (1915), but he also wrote poems all his life. He offers a frank picture of experiences, often dealing with those that others would keep hidden.

He was born at Eastwood, a coal-mining village near Nottingham. He was always sensitive about people and studied his parents' uneasy marriage carefully. His mother felt she had lost social status by marrying a coal-face worker. She disliked her husband's drinking, which took up too much of his wage. Lawrence sided with his mother and tried to describe her life in a poem sequence, *Harmonies and Discords*, which includes *Discord in childhood* (below). A 'huge old ash tree' in front of the family house caught the force of the wind across the valley. The sound of this and parental quarrels downstairs frightened the children.

Discord in childhood

Outside the house an ash-tree hung its terrible
                                                              whips,
And at night when the wind arose, the lash of
                                                     the tree
Shrieked and slashed the wind, as a ship's
Weird rigging[1] in a storm shrieks hideously.

Within the house two voices arose in anger, a
                                                         slender lash
Whistling delirious[2] rage, and the dreadful sound
Of a thick lash booming and bruising, until it
                                                              drowned
The other voice in a silence of blood, 'neath the
                                        noise of the ash.

[1] ropes that control sails and hold them in place   [2] wild

What might the quarrel be about? How does it end?

In *Sons and Lovers* Lawrence says of his mother's voice: 'she wielded the lash unmercifully'. He uses this idea to invent comparisons to describe the parents' voices in this poem. What are they?
The poem is full of violent words. Find them and say which is most impressive.

W What might the father say later about this incident? And the mother? And the children?

The uneasy Lawrence family: David Herbert stands between his parents.

Piano

Softly, in the dusk, a woman is singing to me;
Taking me back down the vista[1] of years, till I see
A child sitting under the piano, in the boom of
                              the tingling strings
And pressing the small, poised[2] feet of a mother
                              who smiles as she sings.

In spite of myself, the insidious mastery[3] of song
Betrays me back, till the heart of me weeps to belong
To the old Sunday evenings at home, with winter
                              outside
And hymns in the cosy parlour,[4] the tinkling
                              piano our guide.

So now it is vain for the singer to burst into
                              clamour[5]
With the great black piano appassionato.[6] The
                              glamour
Of childish days is upon me, my manhood is cast
Down in the flood of remembrance, I weep like
                              a child for the past.

[1] view [2] still but ready to move [3] treacherous power
[4] living room [5] loud noise [6] full of strong emotion

Lawrence's sister recalled how 'some of our happiest hours were spent at our old piano with its faded green silk front. It had to be touched gently to bring out the tinkling notes!'

In the first line Lawrence is an adult. What is happening?
How is past time described in line 2?
What memories does the sound of the piano call up in Lawrence in the first two verses?
Which words in the second verse suggest that he does not want to remember?
Why is 'winter outside' such a strong **PHRASE**?
What happens in the third verse?
Why is Lawrence's 'manhood ... cast/Down' by these memories?

D Discuss the manuscript of the first draft of the poem (below). What differences in wording and ideas are there? What extra information about the singer and the Lawrence family can you find? Explain why Lawrence made the changes he did. How do they improve the poem?

Manuscript draft of Piano.

A *winter's tale*

Yesterday the fields were only grey with scattered
                                          snow,
And now the longest grass-leaves hardly emerge;
Yet her deep footsteps mark the snow, and go
On towards the pines at the hill's white verge.[1]

I cannot see her, since the mist's pale scarf
Obscures[2] the dark wood and the dull orange sky;
But she's waiting, I know, impatient and cold, half
Sobs struggling into her frosty sigh.

Why does she come so promptly, when she must
                                          know
She's only the nearer to the inevitable farewell?
The hill is steep, on the snow my steps are slow –
Why does she come, when she knows what I
                                  have to tell?

[1] edge   [2] blocks out

This poem is about Lawrence breaking up with
his first girlfriend, Jessie Chambers. Pressure from
his mother forced him to make the break before
the relationship moved on to marriage.

Lawrence's mother in her last illness.

Describe the setting briefly. Why does Lawrence
include the snow, mist, twilit sky and dark wood?
Why was the woman first to arrive at the meeting
place?
How does the poet imagine her as she waits?
Why does the hill feel so steep to Lawrence?

W Imagine the woman's thoughts about the scene
and the meeting. Describe the actual meeting.

In 1910 the triumph of Lawrence's first published
novel, *The White Peacock*, was overshadowed by
his mother falling ill with cancer. He was able to
show her the book before she died in December. It
was a stunning blow. In his grief, he almost died
himself. Many poems record the trauma.

ELEGY

The sun immense and rosy
Must have sunk and become extinct
The night you closed your eyes for ever against me.

Grey days, and wan, dree[1] dawnings
Since then, with fritter of flowers –
Day wearies me with its ostentation[2] and fawnings.[3]

Still, you left me the nights,
The great dark glittery window,
The bubble hemming[4] this empty existence with
                                          lights.

Still in the vast hollow
Like a breath in a bubble spinning
Brushing the stars, goes my soul, that skims the
                          bounds[5] like a swallow!

I can look through
The film of the bubble night, to where you are.
Through the film I can almost touch you.

[1] pale, dreary   [2] show designed to impress   [3] attempts
to get attention and praise   [4] edging   [5] limits

How does Lawrence feel about the natural world since
his mother's death?
What has happened to the sun?
What is a 'fritter of flowers'?
With what qualities is the day linked in the sixth line?
Lawrence finds consolation at night. What do darkness
and light represent in the third verse?
How does Lawrence see his soul?
Where is his mother now?

W Examine the bubble idea of the last three verses
and try to explain it.

Lawrence studied at Nottingham University to
become an elementary school teacher. In 1908 he
moved to Croydon near London to be an assistant
at Davidson Road Boys' School. He found the work
difficult: 'School is a conflict – mean and miserable
... the lads and I have a fight ... I struggle with my

The Edwardian classroom with large numbers and rigid discipline.

nature and my class till I feel frayed into rags'. Lawrence described his teaching work in a sequence of poems called *The Schoolmaster*.

Last lesson of the afternoon

When will the bell ring, and end this weariness?[1]
How long have they tugged the leash,[2] and
                                    strained apart,
My pack of unruly[3] hounds! I cannot start
Them again on a quarry[4] of knowledge they hate
                                    to hunt,
I can haul[5] them and urge them no more.

No longer now can I endure the brunt[6]
Of the books that lie out on the desks; a full
                                    threescore[7]
Of several insults of blotted pages, and scrawl
Of slovenly[8] work that they have offered me.
I am sick, and what on earth is the good of it all?
What good to them or me, I cannot see!

                        So, shall I take
My last dear fuel of life to heap on my soul
And kindle[9] my will to a flame that shall consume[10]
Their dross[11] of indifference;[12] and take the toll[13]
Of their insults in punishment? – I will not! –

I will not waste my soul and my strength for this.
What do I care for all that they do amiss![14]
What is the point of this teaching of mine, and of
                                    this
Learning of theirs? It all goes down the same abyss.[15]

What does it matter to me, if they can write
A description of a dog, or if they can't?
What is the point? To us both, it is all my aunt![16]
And yet I'm supposed to care, with all my might.

I do not, and will not; they won't and they don't;
                        and that's all!
I shall keep my strength for myself; they can
                        keep theirs as well.
Why should we beat our heads against the wall
Of each other? I shall sit and wait for the bell.

[1] tiredness   [2] lead   [3] difficult to control   [4] target of a
hunt   [5] drag   [6] bear the main force   [7] 60 (a score = 20)
[8] careless and untidy   [9] set on fire   [10] destroy
[11] useless waste   [12] lack of interest   [13] pay the price
[14] wrong   [15] very deep hole   [16] a lot of nonsense

Describe the class. How have they done their task?
In what state is the class?
Collect some of the unfavourable (pejorative) words that build up the poem's mood.
The poem is written as if Lawrence is speaking his thoughts. Pick out **COLLOQUIAL** words and phrases that create this effect.
What comparisons does Lawrence use for the boys and for his own strength?
What does this poem say about teaching and learning?

W Write Lawrence's diary entry describing his thoughts about his day at school.

W Using several of Lawrence's poems, write about the experiences he describes, commenting on the effects of his **STYLE** and language.

30 Edward Thomas (1878-1917): Memory, time and war

When he left Oxford University in 1899, Thomas became a journalist and influential reviewer, and also wrote prose descriptions of the English countryside. Despite a happy marriage, he was tormented by a sense of failure. A turning point came in 1914 when he met the American poet, Robert Frost (1874-1963), who was living in England and persuaded Thomas to turn to poetry: 'At that moment he was writing as good poetry as anyone alive, but in prose form ... I dragged him out from under the heap of his own work in prose he was buried alive under'. The result was the 'undamming' of Thomas's poetry. During the next three years, he poured out 170 poems before his death in the Battle of Arras in France.

In the summer of 1914 Thomas was travelling by train to see Frost in Gloucestershire, when the express stopped unusually at the tiny station near the Cotswold village of Adlestrop. Thomas caught the moment in a notebook word sketch:

> A glorious day ... we stopped at Adlestrop, through the willows could be heard a chain of blackbirds' songs at 12.45 and one thrush and no man seen, only a hiss of engine letting off steam ... banks of long grass, willowherb and meadowsweet, extraordinary silence between two periods of travel – looking out on grey dry stones between metals and the shining metals and over it all the elms willows and long grass – one man clears his throat – a greater than rustic silence ... Stop only for a minute till signal is up.

Early in 1915 he turned this into a poem.

Adlestrop

Yes. I remember Adlestrop –
The name, because one afternoon
Of heat the express-train drew up there
Unwontedly.[1] It was late June.

The steam hissed. Someone cleared his throat.
No one left and no one came
On the bare platform. What I saw
Was Adlestrop – only the name

And willows, willow-herb, and grass,
And meadowsweet, and haycocks dry,
No whit[2] less still and lonely fair
Than the high cloudlets in the sky.

And for that minute a blackbird sang
Close by, and round him, mistier,
Farther and farther, all the birds
Of Oxfordshire and Gloucestershire.

[1] unusually   [2] not a bit

Why does Thomas start with 'Yes'?
What quality of the remembered scene is stressed by the short sentences and the pauses between them?
What does the poet see at the station? Notice how his focus broadens, like a film shot.
What sound does Thomas become aware of in the last verse? What does this tell you about the old pre-1914 countryside?
What is the **THEME** of this poem? Time? Summer? Memory?

D Compare the prose note and the poem. What has been included and left out in the poem? What has been added? Why is the poem better?

W Write your own descriptive poem about a place and time that you remember. Use carefully chosen detail from your five senses. Begin: 'Yes. I remember ...'

Photograph of Edward Thomas.

Old Man was one of Thomas's earliest poems, and his favourite. Old Man is a scented grey-green herb, bushes of which Thomas always grew at his various homes. Its bitter scent reminded him of something: he could not say what. A discussion of the plant becomes a debate about memory and time.

Old Man

Old Man, or Lad's-love, – in the name there's
nothing
To one that knows not Lad's-love, or Old Man,
The hoar[1]-green feathery herb, almost a tree,
Growing with rosemary and lavender.
Even to one that knows it well, the names
Half decorate, half perplex,[2] the thing it is:
At least, what that is clings not to the names
In spite of time. And yet I like the names.

The herb itself I like not, but for certain
I love it, as some day the child will love it
Who plucks a feather from the door-side bush
Whenever she goes in or out of the house.
Often she waits there, snipping the tips and
shrivelling
The shreds at last on to the path,
Thinking, perhaps of nothing, till she sniffs
Her fingers and runs off. The bush is still
But half as tall as she, though it is as old;
So well she clips it. Not a word she says;
And I can only wonder how much hereafter[3]
She will remember, with that bitter scent,
Of garden rows, and ancient damson trees
Topping a hedge, a bent path to a door,
A low thick bush beside the door, and me
Forbidding[4] her to pick.
As for myself,
Where first I met the bitter scent is lost.
I, too, often shrivel the grey shreds,
Sniff them and think and sniff again and try
Once more to think what it is I am remembering,
Always in vain. I cannot like the scent,
Yet I would rather give up others more sweet,
With no meaning, than this bitter one.

I have mislaid[5] the key. I sniff the spray
And think of nothing; I see and I hear nothing;
Yet seem, too, to be listening, lying in wait
For what I should, yet never can, remember:
No garden appears, no path, no hoar-green bush
Of Lad's-love or Old Man, no child beside,
Neither father nor mother, nor any playmate;
Only an avenue, dark, nameless, without end.

[1] grey   [2] confuse   [3] at some time in the future
[4] refusing to allow   [5] lost

The first eight lines about the herb and its names are complicated. How are these lines like memory itself? What is the difference between 'loving' and 'liking' the herb?

The **NARRATOR** watches the child picking and sniffing the herb. What memories will the scent have for her when she is older?
The last section returns to the groping, uncertain style. What is 'the key'?
Why are there so many negatives in the last four lines? What might the 'avenue' be?
Thomas worked hard to perfect the last line:

'only a dark avenue without an end'
(first prose sketch)
'only a dark avenue, without end or name'
(first draft)
'only an avenue dark without end or name'
(second draft)
'only an avenue, dark, nameless, without end'
(final version)

Why is the last version the best?

W Write your own poem or short prose sketch about memories recreated by the sense of smell.

In 1915 Thomas joined the army. When asked why he was going to fight, he picked up a pinch of English soil and said 'literally for this'. He trained as an artillery officer and went to the front in 1917. His war poems are quiet and thoughtful.

The cherry trees

The cherry trees bend over and are shedding
On the old road where all that passed are dead,
Their petals, strewing[1] the grass as for a wedding
This early May morn when there is none to wed.

[1] scattering

Thomas sees the destruction of war in terms of symbols of peace. What are they?
The poem is one carefully built sentence. Which negative word does it lead up to?

In 1916 Thomas was deciding whether to volunteer for front line service. On leave in Hampshire, he watched a horseplough at work in the countryside. A 'head brass' is the decorative horse-brass on the horse's harness. He imagines a conversation with the ploughman, spoken only when the team reaches his end of the field, where Thomas sits, in uniform, on a fallen tree.

As the team's head brass

As the team's head brass flashed out on the turn
The lovers disappeared into the wood.
I sat among the boughs of the fallen elm
That strewed an angle of the fallow,[1] and
Watched the plough narrowing a yellow square
Of charlock.[2] Every time the horses turned
Instead of treading me down, the ploughman
leaned

Upon the handles to say or ask a word,
About the weather, next about the war.
Scraping the share[3] he faced towards the wood,
And screwed along the furrow[4] till the brass
                                        flashed
Once more.
                The blizzard felled the elm whose crest[5]
I sat in, by a woodpecker's round hole,
The ploughman said. 'When will they take it away?'
'When the war's over.' So the talk began –
One minute and an interval of ten,
A minute more and the same interval.
'Have you been out?' 'No.' 'And don't want to,
                                        perhaps?'
'If I could only come back again, I should.
I could spare an arm. I shouldn't want to lose
A leg. If I should lose my head, why, so,
I should want nothing more ... Have many gone
From here?' 'Yes.' 'Many lost?' 'Yes, a good few.
Only two teams work on the farm this year.
One of my mates is dead. The second day
In France they killed him. It was back in March,
The very night of the blizzard, too. Now if
He had stayed here we should have moved the
                                        tree.'
'And I should not have sat here. Everything
Would have been different. For it would have been

Another world.' 'Ay,[6] and a better, though
If we could see all all might seem good.' Then
The lovers came out of the wood again:
The horses started and for the last time
I watched the clods crumble and topple over
After the ploughshare and the stumbling team.

[1] were scattered about on a corner of the land not planted with crops   [2] wild mustard that grows in fields of corn   [3] blade of the plough   [4] mark made in the ground by the plough   [5] top   [6] yes

The poem starts quietly, with a precise picture of the scene and the plough at work. How are the plough and the lovers symbolic in this poem about war?
Look at the conversation in the second verse paragraph. Work out who says what, Thomas or the ploughman. What is the ploughman's attitude to the war? And Thomas's?
What effects has war had on this quiet country place? Which **PHRASE** is ominous in the last sentence? (An alternative title was *The last team*.)

W   Write your own piece contrasting the English countryside with the battle front.

W   Write about the ideas of time, memory and change in Thomas's poems.

The cornfield *(1918) by John Nash echoes the melancholy mood of Thomas's poems about the English countryside.*

31 Wilfred Owen (1893-1918): The pity of War

Owen volunteered for the army in 1915. After a shell burst near him in 1917, he was declared shell-shocked and sent home to be treated at Craiglockhart Hospital in Edinburgh. There he met the well-known war poet, Siegfried Sassoon (1886-1967), who encouraged him to 'sweat your guts out writing poetry'.

Owen returned to the fighting to share the sufferings of front-line soldiers and to show in his writing the pointlessness of war. He was killed on the Western Front in the last week of the First World War (1914-1918). Owen left a small amount of poetry produced in one extraordinary year. He lived to see only four poems in print, but planned a collection for which he drafted a preface:

My subject is War, and the pity of War.
The poetry is in the pity.
All a poet can do today is warn.

Dulce et decorum est

This is one of Owen's first war poems in the **SATIRICAL STYLE** of Sassoon. It is a protest against poisonous gas, the hideous new chemical weapon, first used in 1915. Owen sent the first draft to his mother: 'Here is a gas poem done yesterday ... the famous Latin tag means of course it is sweet and meet to die for one's country. Sweet! And decorous!' (letter: 16 October 1916). The line from the Roman poet Horace was much quoted by civilian war poets, whom Owen and Sassoon hated. The first draft is addressed to Jessie Pope of the *Daily Mail*, who wrote poems supporting the war, and she is 'my friend' in the last section.

Bent double, like old beggars under sacks,
Knock-kneed, coughing like hags, we cursed
                through sludge,
Till on the haunting flares we turned our backs
And towards our distant rest began to trudge.
Men marched asleep. Many had lost their boots
But limped on, blood-shod. All went lame; all
                blind;
Drunk with fatigue;[1] deaf even to the hoots
Of tired, outstripped Five-Nines[2] that dropped
                behind.

Gas! GAS! Quick, boys! – An ecstasy[3] of fumbling,
Fitting the clumsy helmets just in time;
But someone still was yelling out and stumbling,
And flound'ring like a man in fire or lime[4] ...
Dim, through the misty panes and thick green light,
As under a green sea, I saw him drowning.

In all my dreams, before my helpless sight,
He plunges at me, guttering,[5] choking, drowning.

If in some smothering dreams you too could pace
Behind the wagon that we flung him in,
And watch the white eyes writhing in his face,
His hanging face, like a devil's sick of sin;
If you could hear, at every jolt, the blood
Come gargling from the froth-corrupted[6] lungs,
Obscene[7] as cancer, bitter as the cud[8]
Of vile, incurable sores on innocent tongues, –
My friend, you would not tell with such high zest[9]
To children ardent[10] for some desperate glory,
The old Lie: Dulce et decorum est
Pro patria mori.[11]

[1] tiredness [2] shells [3] intense feeling [4] (quicklime, which burns the skin) [5] flickering and about to go out (like a candle) [6] rotted [7] disgusting [8] regurgitated food [9] excitement [10] eager [11] it is sweet and right to die for your country

Pick out words and comparisons that describe the appearance and the exhaustion of the men.
What does 'drunk with fatigue' mean?
What do the words 'Gas! GAS!' suggest about the sudden change in the soldiers?
Why is the man dying in the gas 'guttering'?
When Owen says 'my friend', what does he really mean?
What happens to the Latin motto at the end of the poem?

W Rewrite the story told in the poem as an entry in Owen's diary. Try to include some of the ugly **DICTION** and comparisons used in the poem, and its final message.

D Role play: Owen visits the dead soldier's family to talk about him and his death. What questions does the family ask? What does Owen say? What does he leave out? Then Owen talks over the incident with a fellow soldier. How are his description and tone different?

Owen rejoined his regiment 1917 for home service in Scarborough, Yorkshire. His billet was a hotel room. Beside the 'crusted dark red jewels' of its open fire, he read a newspaper report of a coal-mining disaster. The result was *Miners*, his first published poem (*The Nation*, January 1918).

Trench warfare, 1914-1918. Flanders *(1936) by Otto Dix.*

Miners

There was a whispering in my hearth,[1]
    A sigh of the coal,
Grown wistful[2] of a former earth
    It might recall.[3]

I listened for a tale of leaves
    And smothered ferns,
Frond[4]-forests, and the low sly lives
    Before the fauns.

My fire might show steam-phantoms simmer
    From Time's old cauldron,
Before the birds made nests in summer,
    Or men had children.

But the coals were murmuring of their mine,
    And moans down there
Of boys that slept wry[5] sleep, and men
    Writhing[6] for air.

And I saw white bones in the cinder-shard,[7]
    Bones without number.
Many the muscled bodies charred,[8]
    And few remember.

I thought of all that worked dark pits
    Of war, and died
Digging the rock where Death reputes[9]
    Peace lies indeed.

Comforted years will sit soft-chaired,
    In rooms of amber;

The years will stretch their hands, well-cheered
    By our life's ember;[10]

The centuries will burn rich loads
    With which we groaned,
Whose warmth shall lull their dreaming lids,

    While songs are crooned;
But they will not dream of us poor lads,
    Left in the ground.

[1] fireplace   [2] sadly thoughtful   [3] remember   [4] fern-leaf
[5] disturbed   [6] squirming   [7] broken pieces of partly burnt
coal or wood   [8] blackened by burning   [9] says
[10] burnt remains

In the first three verses Owen watches his open fire.
The coals seem to whisper a story to him. What is it?
The coals then tell another story in the fourth and fifth
verses. What is it, and why is it sad?
How does the idea shift in the sixth verse?
How are peace and coal linked?
Explain the ideas of 'years', 'amber' and 'life's ember' in
the seventh verse.
What is happening in the last two verses?
What do the last two lines mean?
Trace the pattern of **HALF-RHYMES**. through the poem.
Which are most effective?

Futility[1]

This poem may have been based on Owen's first time in the battle line in the bitter winter of 1916-1917.

Move him into the sun –
Gently its touch awoke him once,
At home, whispering of fields half-sown.
Always it woke him, even in France,
Until this morning and this snow.
If anything might rouse[2] him now
The kind old sun will know.

Think how it wakes the seeds –
Woke once the clays of a cold star.
Are limbs, so dear achieved,[3] are sides
Full-nerved, still warm, too hard to stir?
Was it for this the clay grew tall?[4]
– O what made fatuous[5] sunbeams toil[6]
To break earth's sleep at all?

[1] pointlessness [2] wake [3] difficult to build [4] (in the Bible (Genesis 2:7) God made Adam, the first man, from earth) [5] stupid [6] labour

How is the sun seen in the poem? Which words describe it and its effects on life on Earth?
What is the effect of the questions at the end of the poem? How does Owen feel about life and death in his last, angry question?

W Compare the final version with the draft of *Frustration*. Why has Owen made each change? How has he improved the poem?

W Write a commentary on *Futility*, describing what happens in it and showing Owen's thoughts about life and death. Comment on diction, comparisons and half-rhymes.

First draft of Futility: *Owen's manuscript,* Frustration.

---

32 W. B. Yeats (1865-1939): Dreams and realities

Yeats was the finest writer of the 'Irish literary Renaissance' of the late 19th and early 20th centuries. His achievement was recognised when he won the Nobel Prize for Literature in 1923.

His father, who was a painter, encouraged him to write. The family lived mostly in London with holidays at Sligo in West Ireland, where Yeats heard the Irish folk tales he used in his early writing. Yeats went to Dublin School of Art. Having rejected Christianity, he began what became a lifetime of exploration of other beliefs.

In the 1890s Yeats worked to re-establish Irish literature with the help of Lady Augusta Gregory (1852-1932), a wealthy widow. She helped Yeats to introduce new Irish drama. His own poetry of the 1890s was in the dreamy STYLE of the 'Celtic Twilight' (his own PHRASE). Many pieces were dedicated to Maud Gonne, 'the most beautiful woman in Ireland' and an active nationalist, who rejected his several proposals. After 1910 he used a plainer, more realistic style to strong effect in his poems about the Irish Easter Rising of 1916.

Yeats's enthusiasm for Irish nationalism led him to become a Senator of the Irish Free State in 1922. After his marriage in 1917, he lived in a very old stone tower in County Galway. Here he produced the powerful poetry of his maturity, weaving into it his complicated private SYMBOLISM.

The lake isle of Innisfree[1]

I will arise[2] and go now, and go to Innisfree,
And a small cabin build there, of clay and
                              wattles[3] made:
Nine bean-rows will I have there, a hive for the
                              honey-bee,
And live alone in the bee-loud glade.

And I shall have some peace there, for peace
                              comes dropping slow,
Dropping from the veils of the morning to where
                              the cricket sings;
There midnight's all a glimmer, and noon a
                              purple glow,[4]
And evening full of the linnet's[5] wings.

I will arise and go now, for always night and day
I hear lake water lapping with low sounds by the
                              shore;
While I stand on the roadway, or on the
                              pavements grey,
I hear it in the deep heart's core.

[1] (island in Lough Gill, County Sligo)   [2] get up
[3] wooden frames   [4] reflection of heather in water
[5] (type of bird)

This poem began in two ways. The American
writer Henry Thoreau wrote *Walden, or life in the
woods* (1854) about his stay in a hut on an island.

*'This tumult in the clouds': after a painting (1917)
by R. W. Bradford.*

Yeats's father read a passage to his son, who
'planned to live some day in a cottage on a little
island called Innisfree – seeking wisdom'. Secondly,
in London, Yeats was

> walking through Fleet Street very homesick
> [when] I heard a little tinkle of water and saw a
> fountain in a shop window which balanced a
> little ball upon its jet, and began to remember
> lake water. From the sudden remembrance came
> my poem.

(Autobiography)

What will the poet have in his home on the island?
What will be the pleasures of the place?
What are 'the veils of the morning'? Why is 'midnight
all a glimmer'? What is 'the deep heart's core'?
How is city life quickly described as a contrast?

W Write Yeats's letter to Lady Gregory describing a
day on his dream island.

An Irish airman foresees his death

I know that I shall meet my fate
Somewhere among the clouds above;
Those that I fight I do not hate,
Those that I guard I do not love;
My country is Kiltartan Cross,
My countrymen Kiltartan's poor,
No likely end could bring them loss
Or leave them happier than before.
Nor law, nor duty bade[1] me fight,
Nor public men, nor cheering crowds,
A lonely impulse[2] of delight
Drove to this tumult[3] in the clouds;
I balanced all, brought all to mind,
The years to come seemed waste of breath,
A waste of breath the years behind
In balance with this life, this death.

[1] ordered   [2] sudden strong feeling   [3] loud disturbance

Robert Gregory, Lady Gregory's only son, was an
RAF pilot. He was shot down and killed by mistake
by a British pilot in Italy in 1918. Kiltartan Cross
was the village near his home at Coole Park and
Gregory is 'I' in the poem.

What are the airman's thoughts about death in the first
two lines?
For whom is the airman fighting? Will the war help them?
What did not make him volunteer to fight?
What is 'this tumult in the clouds'?
Can you explain Gregory's 'lonely impulse of delight'?
What conclusion does he reach in the last lines?

W Write a last letter from Robert Gregory to his
mother, in which he tries to explain his feelings and
ideas.

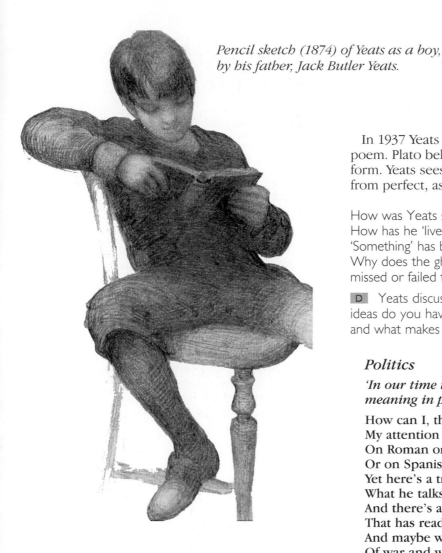

Pencil sketch (1874) of Yeats as a boy, by his father, Jack Butler Yeats.

In 1937 Yeats looked back on his own life in this poem. Plato believed everything had a perfect form. Yeats sees his apparently successful life as far from perfect, as the ghost tells him.

How was Yeats successful at different stages of his life?
How has he 'lived by rule'? What was the 'boyish plan'?
'Something' has been perfected. What is it?
Why does the ghost sing louder? What has the poet missed or failed to do?

D Yeats discusses happiness in this poem. What ideas do you have about the nature of true happiness and what makes a happy life?

Politics

'In our time the destiny of man presents its meaning in political terms.' (Thomas Mann)

How can I, that girl standing there,
My attention fix
On Roman or on Russian
Or on Spanish politics?
Yet here's a travelled man that knows
What he talks about,
And there's a politician
That has read and thought,
And maybe what they say is true
Of war and war's alarms,
But O that I were young again
And held her in my arms!

This poem, written in 1938, is one of Yeats's last. The **EPIGRAPH** from Thomas Mann suggests that, at such a time of crisis as 1938, when events were leading up to the Second World War, writers should write only about political matters. Yeats had read an article containing the Mann quotation, praising him as a poet who did this. Yeats deliberately echoes an old, famous anonymous **LYRIC**, *Westron wind*: 'Christ if my love were in my armes/And I in my bed again'.

Yeats sees himself at a party for important political people. What does he think about the men there and their opinions?
What really interests the poet at the party?
What does Yeats long to be and do?
What is the poet saying is really important in life?

W Write a general commentary on these poems by Yeats, discussing what makes them interesting in subject matter and style.

What then?

His chosen comrades thought at school
He must grow a famous man;
He thought the same and lived by rule,
All his twenties crammed with toil;
'What then?' sang Plato's[1] ghost. 'What then?'

Everything he wrote was read,
After certain years he won
Sufficient[2] money for his need,
Friends that have been friends indeed;
'What then?' sang Plato's ghost. 'What then?'

All his happier dreams came true –
A small old house, wife, daughter, son,
Grounds where plum and cabbage grew,
Poets and Wits[3] about him drew;
'What then?' sang Plato's ghost. 'What then?'

'The work is done,' grown old he thought,
'According to my boyish plan;
Let the fools rage, I swerved in naught,[4]
Something to perfection brought';
But louder sang that ghost, 'What then?'

[1] (Greek thinker) [2] enough [3] writers and thinkers
[4] nothing

REVIEW: GENERAL QUESTIONS ON THE COLLECTION

Spoken activities

1. Working in a group, prepare an assembly session where you introduce some of the poems you have enjoyed in the collection. Each person reads a poem, or part of a poem, with expression, and says something about the poet and the ideas that he or she expresses.

2. Choose a poem that you find interesting and impressive in style and theme. Form a group with others who have also chosen their favourites. Each person reads a poem aloud and makes the case for it being the best. Illustrate closely from the detail of the poems.

3. Choose two similar poems from different eras: two elegies; two love poems; an early and a Romantic sonnet; two poems about city life, the seasons or war, for example. Give a short talk to the class, showing how they are alike and how they differ in style and subject matter.

4. Argue the case for a particular era in poetry being the best. Illustrate carefully from the poems.

5. Give a talk on a favourite poet chosen from those included in this book. Do further research into the poet's life and times, and read and discuss several poems, including perhaps pieces not chosen for this book.

Written activities

Choose at least two poems from different eras to illustrate the following. Discuss the styles, attitudes and historical backgrounds of the poems and poets.

Literary tradition

1. Sonnet: see Wyatt, Shakespeare, Spenser, Donne, Milton, Herbert, Shelley and Barrett Browning.

2. Elegy: see Milton, Gray, Wordsworth, Tennyson, Emily Brontë, Hardy, Lawrence and Owen.

3. Narrative: see Tennyson, Browning, Rossetti and Owen.

4. Love lyric: see Wyatt, Donne, Herrick, Marvell, Wordsworth, Browning, Arnold, Hardy and Lawrence.

Social and historical influences, and cultural contexts

1. Childhood: see Vaughan, Marvell, Coleridge, Hopkins and Lawrence.

2. City life: see Dryden, Pope, Blake, Wordsworth and Yeats.

3. Nature: See Herrick, Burns, Wordsworth, Coleridge, Keats, Hopkins and Thomas.

4. War: see Vaughan, Owen and Yeats.

5. Dreams and memory: see Wyatt, Vaughan, Milton, Coleridge, Byron, Clare, Hardy, Lawrence, Thomas and Yeats.

6. Protest: see Wyatt, Blake, Shelley, Barrett Browning, Lawrence and Owen.

7. Men and women: see Wyatt, Spenser, Herrick/Finch, Marvell, Pope/Chudleigh, Barrett Browning, Browning, Rossetti, Arnold, Hardy and Lawrence.

GLOSSARY

allegory (adj. allegorical)	A work of art in which the characters and story have moral, political or religious meanings.
alliteration	The repetition of similar CONSONANT sounds, especially at the beginning of words close to each other. 'Wind-wandering weed-winding' is an example of alliteration.
antithesis	The placing together of contrasting ideas, words or PHRASES.
archaism (adj. archaic)	The deliberate use of an old-fashioned word or STYLE.
assonance	The repetition of similar VOWEL sounds in words close together, or in different parts of the same word.
aubade	'Aube' means 'dawn' in French, and an aubade is a poem describing the regret of lovers parting at dawn.
Augustans	English writers of late 17th and early 18th centuries who imitated the STYLE of the writers who lived under the Roman Emperor Augustus (27 B.C.-14 A.D.).
autobiography (adj. autobiographical)	The story of a person's life, written by that person.
ballad	A simple NARRATIVE poem or song, often with a REFRAIN.
blank verse	Unrhymed verse in IAMBIC PENTAMETER.
canon	A list of great works of literature.
classical	Writing that imitates the STYLE and THEMES of ancient Roman and Greek literature.
classics	Latin and Greek, which were much studied at school before the 20th century.
coinage	An invented new word or PHRASE.
colloquial	Language that sounds like everyday, familiar conversation.
conceit	An elaborate, often surprising, comparison or idea that forms the basis of a poem.
consonants	Every letter of the alphabet except a, e, i, o and u, which are VOWELS.
couplet	Two lines of verse next to each other that RHYME and use the same METER.
dialogue	Conversation between two or more people.
diction	The choice and use of words.
dramatic monologue	A poem written from the point of view of a single character, which reveals his or her nature and dramatic situation.
elegy (adj. elegiac)	A sad poem or song, especially one which mourns someone's death.
epic	A long NARRATIVE poem with a grand, heroic THEME.
epigram	A short, witty, and often SATIRICAL poem.
epigraph	A quotation at the beginning of a poem, book or chapter that suggests its THEME.
epistle	A verse letter.
epitaph	A piece of writing about a dead person.
fancy	Before the 19th century, this meant imagination.

foot, feet	A group of at least two syllables, which make up a metrical unit. Each line of verse is composed of these poetic feet, which have various forms.
half-rhyme	**RHYME** in which the **CONSONANTS** are similar, but the **VOWEL** sounds are different, for example, *cold/called*.
heroic couplet	A pair of rhyming lines in **IAMBIC PENTAMETER**.
hexameter	A line of verse with six **FEET** (see **METER**).
hyperbole	Deliberate exaggeration for effect.
iambic pentameter	A line of poetry with five iambs (**FEET**), each of which has an unstressed syllable followed by a stressed syllable, for example: 'Who list her hunt, I put him out of doubt' (underlined words are stressed).
image	A mental picture or idea created by descriptive language.
internal rhyme	Words that **RHYME** within a line of verse.
irony (adj. ironic)	A way of using words so that they mean the opposite of what they normally mean.
Jacobean	'Jacobus' means 'James' in Latin; 'Jacobean' therefore refers to the reign of King James I (1603-1625).
lament	A poem or song in which sorrow over a death is expressed.
lyric	A short poem expressing thoughts and feelings.
metaphor	An indirect or suggested comparison (without the words 'like' or 'as'). 'The glorious lamp of heaven, the sun' is an example of a metaphor.
meter	The way in which verse is arranged into a pattern using stressed and unstressed syllables to form **FEET**. Different meters have names that describe the number of feet in a line, for example, **TETRAMETER** (4), **PENTAMETER** (5) and **HEXAMETER** (6).
monologue	A long speech by one person.
motif	An **IMAGE** or idea that is used more than once.
narrative	A narrative is a story. A narrative poem is one that tells a story.
narrator	The person who tells a story.
octave	The first eight lines of a Petrarchan **SONNET**.
octosyllabic (adj.)	This describes a line of verse with eight syllables in it.
ode	A long **LYRIC** poem with a complicated **METER**, expressing thoughts and feelings.
onomatopoeia	The use of words that imitate sounds.
oxymoron	The placing close together of ideas that contradict each other.
parable	A short story that teaches or explains a moral or religious idea.
paradox	An apparently ridiculous or self-contradictory statement, which may still be true.
pathetic fallacy	This is when landscapes and objects that are not alive are shown as having human feelings and moods.
pentameter	A line of verse with five **FEET** (see **METER**).
personification	The representation of an emotion, quality or idea as a human figure.

phrase	A group of words that contains an idea and is part of a sentence.
Poet Laureate	Official poet to the British king or queen.
pun	The use of more than one meaning of a word, or of a word that sounds like another word. The use of the word 'hart' to mean both 'heart' and 'female deer' is an example of a pun.
quatrain	A group of four lines of verse, which may be **RHYMED** or unrhymed.
refrain	A short part of a poem or song that is repeated, usually at the end of a **STANZA**.
rhyme	Words that rhyme end with the same sound. Usually the **VOWELS** in the rhyming words are the same, and the **CONSONANTS** change, for example, *cold/bold*. Rhymes are sometimes used in poems, usually at the end of lines. (See also **HALF-RHYME** and **INTERNAL RHYME**.) **SONNETS** have fixed rhyme schemes.
Romantic	An artistic movement in the late 18th century and the early 19th: nature, human imagination and feelings are the key Romantic **THEMES**.
satire (adj. satirical)	Attacking ideas, people or society using mockery.
sestet	The last six lines of Petrarchan **SONNET**.
simile	A comparison in which one thing is compared to another, usually using the words 'as' or 'like'. 'My heart is like a singing bird' is an example of a simile.
sonnet	A 14-line poem in **IAMBIC PENTAMETER** with **RHYMES**. The rhymes are arranged in one of several patterns. An Italian or Petrarchan sonnet, which is made up of an **OCTAVE** and a **SESTET**, rhymes either *abbabba cde cde*, or *abbabba cdcdcd*. An English sonnet is made up of three **QUATRAINS** and a **COUPLET**. The Spenserian sonnet rhymes *abab bcbc cdcd ee*, and the Shakespearean sonnet rhymes *abab cdcd efef gg*.
stanza	A verse or group of lines of poetry that form a unit within a poem.
style	The way in which a writer expresses ideas.
symbol	An object, person or idea that stands for or suggests something else.
tetrameter	A line of verse with four **FEET**.
theme	An idea that is repeated or developed in a poem.
tone	The poet's manner, mood and attitude.
verse form	The shape and pattern of lines or **STANZAS** in a poem.
vowels	The letters a, e, i, o and u.

USEFUL BACKGROUND MULTIMEDIA MATERIAL

Individual poets: the Dent Everyman editions are most useful for the younger student

English Poetry Plus: CD-ROM (Chadwyck-Healy, 1995)
   5,000 poems by 314 poets, with background

Stephen Coote, *The Penguin Short History of English Literature* (Penguin, 1993)
   Excellent, up-to-date general survey

J. Cuddon, *A Dictionary of Literary Terms* (Penguin, 1977)
   Valuable reference of technical terms of poetry

R. Miller and R. Greenberg, *Poetry: An Introduction* (Macmillan, 1981)
   Useful introduction to forms and technicalities

Six Centuries of Verse: Three Videos (Trumedia)
   Outstanding television series and illustrated book

Anthony Thwaite, *Six Centuries of Verse* (James Methuen, 1984)

English verse: Thomas Wyatt to Wilfred Owen, (Penguin Audiobooks, 1995)
   Six audio cassettes

INDEX OF POETS

INDEX OF TITLES

INDEX OF FIRST LINES